The Sherlock Holmes Scrapbook

The Sherlock Scrapbo

Holmes

Fifty years of occasional articles, newspaper cuttings, letters, memoirs, anecdotes, pictures, photographs and drawings relating to the great detective

EDITED BY PETER HAINING

Editorial Consultant G. Ken Chapman

FOREWORD BY PETER CUSHING

NEW ENGLISH LIBRARY
TIMES MIRROR

Foreword

"Everything comes in circles . . .
The old wheel turns and the same
spoke comes up. It has all been
done before and will be again . . ."
Thus spake the Master to Inspector
Alec MacDonald in "The Valley of
Fear". Such a lot has been written
already about Sherlock Holmes
that some may be inclined to say —
surely not *another* volume? But the
old axiom "You cannot have too
much of a good thing" can be
applied with emphasis in this
particular case.

Peter Haining's "Scrapbook" is
a sheer delight for aficionados and
novices alike, and the uninitiated
(if, indeed, there are any) will soon
become enthusiasts once they clap
eyes upon this enchanting
compilation.

With the vast wealth of material
at his disposal it might be thought
that Mr. Haining's task has been an
easy one; all he had to do was dip

PETER CUSHING, apart from being an expert on Sherlock Holmes, is
also widely recognised as the finest modern portrayer of the Master on
films and television. Indeed experts voted his recent performance in the
film of "The Hound of the Baskervilles" as the second best of all time,
closely following that of the legendary Eille Norwood. Mr. Cushing has
been an enthusiastic devotee of the Great Detective since his youth and
now owns over sixty books on the subject, including many copies of the
rare "Strand Magazine" containing the original Holmes' serialisation.

First published in Great Britain by New English Library, Barnard's Inn,
Holborn, London EC1 in 1973.

Revised and corrected second edition 1974.

Copyright © 1973 by Peter Haining. All rights reserved.

Designed by Michael Osborn

Printed in Great Britain by Tinling (1973) Ltd.,
Prescot, Lancs. (a member of the Oxley printing Group).

450 01397 9

in with both hands, as it were, and scatter his findings haphazardly upon the following pages. But like all things well done, the loving care he has taken in selection and connotation gives little indication of the enormous amount of research and hard work that has gone into this collection, and it leaves the reader hungry for more, which is always the best way to leave the table, looking forward to the next meal after due digestion.

E. V. Knox once wrote an Obituary Notice on the passing of Sherlock Holmes, which was originally published in the "Strand Magazine", while his brother Father Ronald A. Knox, suggested in his "Essays in Satire", that one might some day look about for Holmes in Heaven, forgetting that he was only a character in a book.

Be that as it may, the great detective is immortal. Thanks to Peter Haining "The Sherlock Holmes Scrapbook" will do much to perpetuate this belief, bringing pleasure to all who read it, and may I hope that they will cling, as I do, to the sentiment expressed by Vincent Starrett —

". . . there can be no grave for Sherlock Holmes or Watson . . . Shall they not always live in Baker Street? Are they not there this instant as one writes? . . . Outside, the hansoms rattle through the rain, and Moriarty plans his latest devilry. Within, the sea-coal flames upon the hearth, and Holmes and Watson take their well-won ease . . . So they still live for all that love them well: in a romantic chamber of the heart: in a nostalgic country of the mind: where it is always 1895."

Peter Cushing
Whitstable, Kent
1973

BEETON'S·CHRISTMAS·ANNUAL

A STUDY IN SCARLET

By A. CONAN DOYLE

Containing · also
Two Original
DRAWING ROOM PLAYS.

I

FOOD FOR POWDER.
By R. ANDRE

← 2 →

THE FOUR LEAVED SHAMROCK
By C. J. HAMILTON

WITH ENGRAVINGS
By D H FRISTON
MATT STRETCH,
AND
R. ANDRÉ

WARD·LOCK·&·CO
LONDON·NEW·YORK
·AND·MELBOURNE·

Introduction

Sherlock Holmes makes his debut.
Left: The cover of the now extremely rare edition of "Beeton's Christmas Annual" for December 1887 which contained the first adventure of the Great Detective. A copy of the magazine was recently sold at Sotheby's for £480, but Conan Doyle himself only received an outright payment of £25 for the story!
Above: This illustration from the "Annual" is the very first to depict Holmes in action. It shows the Master examining a clue with Inspectors Lestrade and Gregson — Watson is the top-hatted figure at the rear. The artist was D.H. Friston.

"Holmes was a drug addict without a single amiable trait."
George Bernard Shaw

"Sherlock Holmes is the W.G. Grace of the Detective story."
Julian Symons

Sherlock Holmes is without doubt the most famous character in the literature of crime. He is the epitomy of the man of reason, the archetypal investigator and the master of detectives. It has been argued, with some justification, that he stands with only two other fictional characters — Hamlet and Robinson Crusoe — in being familiar to readers all over the world.

Holmes is a true phenomenon; a man whose adventures have delighted generation after generation of readers, and whose *modus operandi* has become the standard of achievement for perhaps the most widely read genre in contemporary fiction. The novelist Norman Collins has provided what is for me the most succinct description of this amazing development:

"It is generally agreed that the detective story was invented by an American, Edgar Allan Poe. But it was an Englishman,(or rather an Irishman of Scottish birth), Arthur Conan Doyle, who borrowed the formula, mixed in a little Frenchman, Gaboriau, and set the pattern for a whole host of imitators. What Conan Doyle did was simply tremendous; he made his principal character, Sherlock Holmes, into that extraordinary thing, a household word. And indeed, the fame of his character haunted him: throughout his long life, Conan Doyle was in the strange position of being a man pursued by his own detective."

The basis for this legend lies in the fifty-six short stories and four novels which Doyle wrote about Holmes and his faithful assistant and chronicler, Dr. Watson, between 1881 and the advent of the First World War. The cult of Holmes, for such it soon was and still is, was not long in developing; for no sooner had the disenchanted author attempted to 'rid himself of the troublesome detective' over the Reichenbach Falls in 1893, than he was assaulted with such a barrage of complaints that he was forced to restore him to life.

The actual study of Holmes and his cases from an analytical point of view followed not long after this with an essay written by Father Ronald Knox in 1911. A veritable library of papers, articles and treatises have filled the intervening years until the present time, when there would seem to be few obscure points in any of the cases or debatable statements made by the two men in conversation, which have not been probed and analysed from every viewpoint. (Such is the magnetism of Holmes, however, that there will probably be found still more!)

Not every Doyle reader has been swept along in this tide of adulation, though. Christopher Isherwood, for one, found Holmes "one of the truly great comic characters of our literature . . . he is the classic caricature of the Amateur Detective in whose person the whole art of detection is made ridiculous." The Sherlockian expert, Bernard Darwin, (how appropriate a name!) was less scathing when writing in 1959, but still found himself "tired of these ingenious games clever people play with one another over Holmes." He wrote simply, "I have had enough of this great Holmes joke. I want to go back to the simple and sublime jokes which are the stories themselves."

Whichever approach to the canon is to your taste, there can be no denying that 'The Great Detective' figure emerged in this country in the shape of Sherlock Holmes and having flourished until the 1930s, declined with the Second World War. "It is a remarkable fact," the crime writer and critic, Julian Symons has noted, "that in the work of the British crime novelists who have come into prominence since the war there is not a single Great Detective to be found."

So what is the magic of this man who has attracted such fervent and continuing admiration on a world-wide scale? Who has been the subject of innumerable films, stage plays, television serials, radio broadcasts, records, advertisements, competitions, games, crossword puzzles and even posthumous sequels? Is it, as Edgar Smith, an American admirer and editor of the "Baker Street Journal" has put it, "the appeal of the half-remembered, half-forgotten times of smug Victorian illusion, of gaslit comfort and contentment, of perfect dignity and grace"? Or much more simply the involvement with a kind of absorbing, unselfconcious storytelling now sadly no longer produced? Again, the answer is not a simple one and writers of the stature of A.A. Milne, Anthony Boucher, Frank Swinnerton, Dorothy L. Sayers, John Dickson Carr and Irving Wallace are just a few of those who have attempted solutions.

Perhaps I may venture to suggest that at least part of the answer rests in what has been written about Holmes and in those to whom he has become, in truth, a real person. With this in mind, THE SHERLOCK HOLMES SCRAPBOOK has been assembled to mirror the fascination with, and the fantastic appeal of, The Great Detective of Baker Street.

This book, it should be stressed right from the outset, does not pretend to be exhaustive nor to contain material relevent to every tiny detail of the adventures. It is merely an attempt to bring together a wide-ranging amount of popular material from the great years of a developing phenomenon which, if anything, seems to be gaining still more strength today.

Pictorial matter has been given especial prominence in the book, for this seems to me to have received least attention in most other works on Holmes. (The exception, of course, being the classic "Annotated Sherlock Holmes" compiled by William S. Baring-Gould which contains all the illustrations from the original publication of the stories and novels.) We have also dug deeply to find forgotten news items, obscure letters and amusing anecdotes to round out the picture. This has, inevitably, led to the omission of one or two of the noted Sherlockian writers, but may I plead justification on the grounds that this is a book aimed at the general reader as much, if not more, than the devotee?

I feel it is also important to mention here to the expert that I have tried not to unduly duplicate the articles and illustrations already widely reprinted, and to this end you will find only a handful of Sydney Paget's classic illustrations from the "Strand Magazine" and little if anything from the English "Sherlock Holmes Journal" or the American "Baker Street Journal."

In a nutshell, then, this book is an attempt to show something of the extent of the Legend of Sherlock Holmes. It has drawn on the popular media (newspapers, magazines, journals and the broadcasting publications) and it is my hope that for those who are new to the Adventures, it will serve both as an introduction to them and guide to those authorities who can interpret their intricacies and dramas in still more detail. For those who are already familiar with the "wonder world", I hope it will prove an interesting and, in the main, fresh look at Holmes and Dr. Watson.

Finally, may I close with a message by Ben Abramson, the revered New York bookseller and doyen among Sherlockians, which seems so appositely to sum up the cordiality I have found among the lovers of Conan Doyle's works: "My Irregular and sincere greetings and best wishes that this will be for you a Happy Holmesian year; that Dukes of Holdernesse will pay you fat fees; that you will always find the missing three-quarter and that there will always be both a Mary Morstan and a Doctor Watson for you."

PETER HAINING
Birch Green, Essex
April 1973

SHERLOCK HOLMES

MISS MARY MORSTAN

DR. WATSON

SHERLOCK HOLMES DISGUISED

IRENE ADLER

DR. GRIMESBY ROYLOTT

POLLY HINTON

MOTHER SUPERIOR

LESTRADE

MISS STAPLETON

JEFFERSON HOPE

DAME ERMYNTRUDE LORING

MISS VIOLET HUNTER

PROFESSOR MORIARTY

MAN WITH TWISTED LIP

REBECCA TAYLFORTH

BRIGADIER GERARD

MISS HELEN STONER

KING OF BOHEMIA

MISS HATTY DORAN

LUCY FERRIER

TONGA

SIR NIGEL LORING

HOUND OF THE BASKERVILLES

MR. JABEZ WILSON

Sherlock Holmes~ a short biography

HOLMES, Sherlock, private consulting detective; b. Jan. 1854, of family of English country squires; g.g.s. of Carle Vernet, French painter. Educ.: public school; Cambridge University; St. Bartholomew's Hospital, London. Discovered new test for bloodstains, superseding old guaiacum test; in private consultative practice from 1886, disappeared and erroneously reported killed, Reichenbach Falls, Switzerland, 4 May 1891; explored Tibet, under the name of Sigerson, 1891–92, also the Far and Near East; returned to professional practice in London, April 1894, and completed destruction of Professor Moriarty's criminal organisation; retired to small farm near Eastbourne, Sussex, 1903, devoting himself to bee-keeping and philosophy; confidential mission to Shantung for the Admiralty, 1914; undertook (under the name of Altamont) a German espionage case, 1912–14, instrumental in the capture of the international spy, Von Bork; accounts of more celebrated cases edited by Sir Arthur Conan Doyle, the historical novelist, q.v. from notes by Dr. John H. Watson: A Study in Scarlet, 1887; The Sign of the Four, 1890; The Adventures of Sherlock Holmes, 1905; The Valley of Fear, 1915; His Last Bow, 1917; The Case-Book of Sherlock Holmes, 1927. Publications: The Blanched Soldier, The Lion's Mane (accounts of cases); Practical Handbook of Bee Culture with Some Observations on the Segregation of the Queen; numerous technical monographs relating to criminology, music, and scientific subjects; has been working for many years upon a work to focus the whole art of detection into one volume. Recreations: criminology, sensational literature, chemistry, music, the violin, boxing, fencing, baritsu, philosophy, bee-keeping. Address: 221B Baker Street, NW1. Club: Diogenes.

This entry for Who's Who appears with the kind collaboration of the publishers, Messrs. Adam & Charles Black, and the Library Committee for the Borough of St. Marylebone.

Sherlock Holmes as played on the stage by William Gillette and drawn in 1901 by "Spry" for "Vanity Fair". Right: A composite picture of Holmes and some of his most famous cases by Sidney Paget, his most famous illustrator, for "The Strand Magazine".

How S--rl--k H----s solved the Great Face Mystery.

"My dear Watson," said S--rl--k H----s, holding up the little instrument with which he had shaved in less than three minutes, "you know I have received valuable presents from reigning Sovereigns. But from one of the principals in that case which you chronicled as 'The Sprinkled Napkin' I obtained a present which is more useful and in some senses more valuable than anything else I possess. With its help I have reduced my shaving time from a quarter of an hour to three minutes, and have changed a most troublesome and painful business into as simple and pleasant an operation as brushing one's teeth.

"And it has been the key to a mystery that baffled me ever since I dealt with that Stock Exchange case. You will remember we noticed that the men we dealt with were not only well dressed, but that their faces were well shaven and were free from those scratches and cuts which so frequently disfigure the man who shaves himself. I wondered how they managed. Of course, I thought of safety razors, but the only kind I knew were old-fashioned and unsatisfactory — indeed, they were just as bad as an ordinary razor because it was impossible—or at least difficult—to strop them properly. But this clever little Auto-Strop Razor explains everything. The blade of wafer steel is marvellously sharp, and the automatic stropping device enables anyone to keep it in perfect condition without the slightest trouble. Morning after morning I shave myself with the AutoStrop Razor — quickly, comfortably —never cutting myself, never irritating my face or neck. The man who perfected the AutoStrop Safety Razor," said my friend, with a smile, "has rendered a service to his fellow men which can scarcely be over-estimated.

"In going about I have observed that the Auto-Strop Safety Razor, with one dozen AutoStrop blades, special horse-hide strop, all fitted in neat leather case, is on sale in all the shops at the price of £1 1s.—a price which puts it within the reach of every man who has occasion to shave himself or be shaved. I came across it also on the occasion of my recent visit to the Franco-British Exhibition at Stand No. 65, which, as you no doubt know, is opposite the Stadium. I was given to understand also that it was to be seen in the Canadian Building. The Auto-Strop Safety Razor Co., Ltd., are prepared to send their illustrated booklet to anyone, giving full particulars of a special free trial offer they make, so I would suggest," he concluded, "that you send a postcard for a copy, addressing Dept. R., AutoStrop Safety Razor Co., Ltd., 61, New Oxford Street, London, W."

1908

Sherlock Holmes–world figure

I do not remember the first appearance of Sherlock Holmes. When *A Study in Scarlet* was published in *Beeton's Christmas Annual* I was only three years old, and was not six at the time *The Sign of the Four* (as it was then called) appeared in *Lippincott's Magazine*. In July, 1891, when *A Scandal in Bohemia*, the first of Holmes's *Adventures*, made the *Strand Magazine* essential reading for civilized men, I was just in sight of a seventh birthday; and knew nothing of the furore.

How soon Holmes did knock me silly I cannot say; probably *The Hound of the Baskervilles* was the beginning of a lifelong enthusiasm. Nevertheless, William Gillette's play, and what I believe to have been a parody of it at Terry's Theatre, seem again to blaze in electric lights in the Strand. There was somebody in a boys' paper called "Sheerluck Jones"; somebody else called "Chubblock Holmes"; and I think a third monster named something Gnomes. All helped in their depraved way to advertise the original, despite rivalry, as the eighteen nineties advanced, from Arthur Morrison's Martin Hewitt, Robert Barr's Eugene Valmond, and — swamping in wide advertisement every other fictional character of the hour — Guy Boothby's Dr. Nikola.

Dr. Nikola and his golden-eyed black cat could be seen all over London, the cat giving its name to a brand of popular cigarettes, and a long wisp of smoke stretching upward past the doctor's head across every hoarding. Outwardly, then, Dr. Nikola was the great invention; Sherlock Holmes only an occasion of parody. How wrong this was, we now know; at the time I was unaware of its wrongness. The *Strand Magazine* must have been in innumerable houses; it was not ours. On the one side *Chums* and the Aldine boys' publications; on the other Stead's Penny Poets and Novelists. It is probable that through a circulating library, I read *The Refugees* and *Micah Clarke* before attaining the heights of *The Man with the Twisted Lip*. Doyle's romances, indeed, were part of the age, along with *The Prisoner of Zenda*, *A Gentleman of France*, and Gilbert Parker's *When Valmond came to Pontiac*. Every boy from twelve to ninety revelled in *Rodney Stone* and *The Exploits of Brigadier Gerard*.

Yet what thrilling memories of delight return to me at the thought of Sidney Paget's illustrations to the Holmes stories! That picture, recently so much discussed because nobody can comprehend its geography, which shows Holmes and Watson recognizing the bearded villain in the hansom cab, is ever in the mind's eye. So are the scenes of Watson shooting the hound in *The Mystery of the Copper Beeches*, of Holmes in his dressing-gown, of Holmes

lashing at the speckled band with his stick, together with dozens of others. They are as immortal as the stories themselves.

It was Paget's pictures which gave Holmes visual reality for all, which carried him through the world until he became the most universally familiar imaginary figure in two hemispheres. Perhaps John Bull and Uncle Sam, as national emblems, are as recognizable in China; but not Shakespeare, not Dickens, hardly even Cervantes, produced a man who would be acclaimed at sight by so many people. He is known all over the United States. He is known in Russia. Only the other day I found in a Swiss newspaper which came wrapped round some books a story about Holmes solving a mystery — perhaps a political mystery — in Prague; and the drawings illustrating it, although they caricatured the great detective were all based upon Paget's portrait.

So much is Holmes the man depicted by Paget that when a plaque to celebrate the meeting of Watson and Stamford in the Criterion Bar (see *A Study in Scarlet*) was recently unveiled, and Mr. Carleton Hobbs, the actor impersonating Holmes, stepped in costume from a hansom cab, two strangers who happened to be passing glanced at him with interest, and one, quite casually, as if he remarked "There's Winston," said "Oh, it's Sherlock Holmes."

There was no incongruity in this. The man whose words, "You know my methods, Watson," or "Let me recommend your attention . . : to the curious incident of the dog in the night," have passed into current speech with an aura of magic, was, in fact, more than life size. Doyle never fussed to produce an air of strength or inscrutability. The strength, the skill, the vanity were integral to his conception of Holmes. He took from Dr. Bell, the Edinburgh professor, that relish in mystification which was salt to Holmes's analysis. He made Holmes say, now and again, that it might be well for Watson to bring his revolver; thereby revealing his own ineffable courage. He boldly attributed to Holmes statements and pamphlets which besides being scientific were also amusing and stimulating to the amateur. He was brief, direct, and a story-teller. He created Holmes and Watson without ever blurring either of them.

It is this fact of creation, rather than the novelty of Holmes, which accounts for those raging outcries of the public over the lamentable affair of the Reichenbach Falls, and the siege of the book-stalls when *The Empty House* brought Holmes to life again. Plots as ingenious as those of the inferior Holmes stories had been invented and have been invented ever since. What has not been equalled is the confident originality shown by such opening sentences as "It was in the spring of the year 1894" or "I had called upon my friend Sherlock Holmes." These openings at once announce that the two are embarked upon another investigation. All the discussion about what part of Watson's body was damaged, or the number of times he married, merely emphasizes the fact of creation. An inferior writer would have been scrupulously exact in such details. Doyle, with the wealth of a maker, did not thriftily re-read his old yarns. He did not care how many wives or wounds Watson might have had. He was after big game.

The game, fundamentally, was adventure. You can see that in *The Hound of the Baskervilles*. It is sometimes said that Holmes had predecessors, that his methods had been forestalled in the Apocrypha, by Voltaire in *Zadig*, by D'Artagnan in *Le Vicomte de Bragelonne*, and by Edgar Allan Poe in *The Murders in the Rue Morgue*, *The Purloined Letter*, and *The*

Ronald Searle
june 51
221B Baker Street

Mystery of Marie Roget. No doubt Doyle had read all these instances of deduction, as he had read *The Moonstone* and the tales of Gaboriau.

I have read Gaboriau's *Lecoq the Detective, The Gilded Clique,* and a story concerning the murder of an old woman, the name of which I forget. [It was *The Lerouge Case*]. All very good. Wilkie Collins, but more so.

But his first inspirations had occurred long before. He had been impressed and tickled by the "method"

of Dr. Bell, in Edinburgh, who when Doyle was a medical student enjoyed startling his pupils by announcing at sight the trades of incoming patients. He had also longed for a life of activity, which the need of earning money had forced him to limit to the football and cricket fields. Finally, he had an interest in criminology and a grand natural gift for story-telling.

Take of these elements all that is fusible,
Melt them all down in a pipkin of crucible.
Set them to simmer and take off the scum;
And our great Sherlock Holmes is the residuum

"Elementary, my dear Watson," as Holmes did not say.

What Holmes really said to Watson was "You see; but you do not observe." Watson did not know how many stairs led up from Baker Street to their rooms. Holmes knew. The minutiae which Watson and (as a man) Doyle missed were his joy. Holmes remarked what Doyle scribbled hastily in an old notebook:

'The coat-sleeves, the trouser-knee, the callosities of the forefinger and thumb, the boot — any one of these might tell us; but that all united should fail to enlighten the trained observation is incredible.'

If it is true that Doyle himself was not observant, the fact illustrates his genius in *imagining* himself Holmes. This genius caused him to create, and not merely invent, one who was destined to become a world figure. Just so did Cervantes create Don Quixote, or Dumas the three musketeers.

I learned from Mr. Hesketh Pearson's book on Doyle something which confirms the point. Where more ingenious modern writers, of great talent, invent idiosyncrasies for their great detectives, sometimes small clownings, sometimes facetious mannerisms of speech, Doyle, the originator, told us little but what seemed to arise naturally from unlimited knowledge of Holmes. Mr. Pearson quotes from an unpublished story one more detail of a night journey by train which proves this:

'It was one of Holmes characteristics that he could command sleep at will. Unfortunately he could resist it at will also, and often and often have I had to remonstrate with him on the harm he must be doing himself when deeply engrossed in one of his strange or baffling problems he would go for several consecutive days and nights without one wink of sleep. He put the shades over the lamps, leant back in his corner, and in less than two minutes his regular breathing told me he was fast asleep. Not being blessed with the same gift myself, I lay back in my corner for some time nodding to the rhythmical throb of the express as it hurled itself forward through the darkness. Now and again as we shot through some brilliantly illuminated station or past a line of flaming furnaces, I caught for an instant a glimpse of Holmes' figure coiled up snugly in the far corner with his head sunk upon his breast.'

Do you not see the scene? The anxious exasperation of Watson at his friend's willpower? The secret of his loyalty? It is all in that description, so bare, so undistinguished in style, yet so free from fanciful adulteration. Having created Holmes, Doyle could not go wrong. As for ourselves, that is why we cannot have enough of him.

The many facets of Dr. Watson

" 'A middle-sized, strongly built man — square jaw — thick neck. A mask over his eyes.'

" 'That's rather vague,' said Sherlock Holmes. 'Why, it might be a description of Watson.'

" 'It's true,' said the Inspector. 'It might be a description of Watson.' "

And so it was, as a perusal of *The Six Napoleons* will show. The unfolding of the inner man, the Watson behind the mask, was only finished with the completion of the series, and as a work of art it far excelled the creation of Sherlock Holmes himself. What a trusty old creature he was — Watson, who kept a bull pup, who smoked ships' tobacco, who enjoyed Beaune with his lunch, who disliked getting up in the morning, who used to play Rugby for Blackheath, whom Holmes — in *The Abbey Grange* — summed up with that ruthless terseness which is one of his chief claims for our regard:

"See here, Captain Croker, we'll do this in due form of law. You are prisoner. Watson, you are a British jury, and I never met a man who was more eminently fitted to represent one."

Yes, we know almost everything that there is to know about Watson. How he took his degree of Doctor of Medicine of the University of London, how he became an Army Surgeon, how he was wounded in Afghanistan and invalided out of the Army on pension, and how there now lies "somewhere in the vaults of the bank of Cox and Co., at Charing Cross, a travel-worn battered tin despatch box bearing the name John H. Watson, M.D., late Indian Army." But the fact that there was also a Mrs. Watson is not so widely realised, though Holmes commented on her existence somewhat acidly:

"The good Watson had at that time deserted me for a wife, the only selfish action I can recall in our association. I was alone."

And it is in this that we begin to suspect less transparent parts in the good doctor: that same despatch box is one of the causes of our uneasiness. Watson was the sort of person who would work the "travel-worn battered tin despatch box" for all it was worth: his service abroad was very short, and it is extremely unlikely that he took the despatch box with him to Afghanistan: one voyage to India and back should not have made it so very travel-worn or battered. He gave the information about it in *Thor Bridge*, and, we ask, why "Indian Army"? For in *A Study in Scarlet* he described himself as "late of the Army Medical Department," and states that he was attached to the Fifth Northumberland Fusiliers as Assistant Surgeon, and afterwards was posted to the Berkshires, with whom he was wounded? And why John? In *The Man with the Twisted Lip*, Mrs. Watson, addressing an old school friend, said—

" . . . now you will have some wine and water, and sit here comfortably and tell us all about it. Or would you rather that I sent James off to bed?"

"James" was the Watson we know: how can he explain this?

Sir A. Conan Doyle was guilty of two errors of judgement, not only in attempting to finish off Holmes at the Reichenbach Fall on 4th May, 1891, but also in letting Watson get married. This was mere carelessness, of course. Watson should not have been allowed to entangle himself with a young woman when all his time was dedicated to Holmes; the author should have been much more firm with the young man. The only excuse that can be made is that it was not then clear how firm a hold the pair had taken on the public mind. The attempted disposal of Holmes down the Reichenbach was a serious and deliberate attempt by his creator to rid himself of a fellow who had become a menace to him, as well as being a frightful bore. But when Holmes proved too slippery for his maker, and the author decided to extricate him from the perilous foothold on which he was lodged, Sir Arthur also decided to be thoroughly ruthless and put Mrs. Watson out of the way. It was brutal murder, but it had to be done. It was no good pretending that Mrs. Watson would sit by and see John — or James, as she called him, poor woman — set out light-heartedly with his Army revolver in his pocket, at any hour of the day or night. This, for example, was a sample of what went on, an extract from a conversation in a Portsmouth train between Holmes and Watson, who was then a practitioner in Paddington.

" 'To-day must be a day of enquiries.'

" 'My practice —— ' I began.

" 'Oh, if you find your own cases more interesting than mine,' said Holmes, with some asperity.

" 'I was going to say, my practice could get along very well for a day or two.' "

And this "in the July succeeding my marriage"! Things got worse, of course, after such a beginning. "One Sunday morning I received one of Holmes' laconic messages: 'Come if convenient — if inconvenient come all the same. — S.H.' "

No woman, not even one who could marry Watson, would put up with that. It was a choice between Watson's wife and Holmes, and Holmes, after all, was the breadwinner, so poor Mrs. Watson had to go. We are not told the details of her going. Watson was not the kind to parade his grief in public: the only reference to the matter is in April, 1894, when Holmes reappeared *(The Empty House).*

"In some manner he had learned of my own sad bereavement, and his sympathy was shown in his manner rather than in his words.

"'Work is the best antidote for sorrow, my dear Watson, and I have a piece of work for both of us to-night—— ' "

The man was incorrigible. So the partnership was resumed without let or hindrance, and Holmes gave an unexpected sign of generosity.

"At the time of which I speak Holmes had been

doctor, *The Sign of Four* tells all that is known of his wife. Watson met Mary Morstan in 1888. She was then twenty-seven, an orphan, the daughter of a captain in the Indian Army, she had been educated in Edinburgh, and was then governess for the children of a Mrs. Cecil Forrester; they appear to have been married in the spring of 1889. Watson had shared the rooms at 221B Baker Street with Holmes from 1888, but shortly before his marriage he bought a practice in Paddington from "old Mr. Farquhar" who, suffering from St. Vitus Dance, had let the receipts drop from about £1,500 to £300 a year; another doctor named Anstruther lived

Illustration: Frank Wiles 1888

STOP HIM HOLMES! SMASH THE TEST TUBE!

Illustration: Frank Giacoia 1955

back some months and I, at his request, had sold my practice and returned to share the old quarters at Baker Street. A young doctor named Verner had purchased my small Kensington practice, and given with astonishingly little demur the highest price I ventured to ask — an incident which only explained itself some years later, when I found that Verner was a distant relation of Holmes', and that it was my friend who really found the money. . . . "

How long the second partnership lasted we are not told, nor what finally became of Watson. In *The Lion's Mane*, Holmes, then a bee-farmer, records——

" . . . my withdrawal to my Sussex home, when I had given myself up entirely to that soothing life of Nature for which I had so often yearned during the long years spent in the gloom of London. At the present period of my life, July, 1907, the good Watson had passed almost beyond my ken. An occasional week-end visit was the most I ever saw of him."

After this brief outline of history we may turn back for more details of the Watsons. While *A Study in Scarlet* gives most of the biographical details about the

next door to the Watsons. There is some doubt about Watson's income during his residence with Holmes, for he seems to have had no means apart from his half-pay He emphasises the fact that Holmes frequently worked for no remuneration, but some rich prizes are recorded — he received one thousand pounds from the King of Bohemia (£300 in gold, £700 in notes), six thousand pounds from the Duke of Holdernesse, and five hundred pounds from von Bork. Other large sums must also have come to him by the nature of his cases, though Watson omits to mention them; probably he was not told: but no part of this spoil comes to the good Watson. Of course, if it is to be understood that the profits of his memoirs are to be calculated at the ordinary rates, his financial position would be satisfactory, and as a writer Watson took himself seriously. The unexpected touchiness he displays at any criticism of his literary efforts was the legitimate pride of an artist, for from the *Study in Scarlet* to the *Case Book* the writing in the memoirs is on a uniformly high standard. It is this quality, added to the skilful revelation of the character of the narrator, that has made the series live through a revolution in the science of the detection of crime and an ever-increasing avalanche of detective fiction. Of these, the two outstanding character-figures which the literature of our time has produced, the personality of Watson becomes all the more permanent as some of the gloss falls from the figure of his patron. "Good old Watson!" Holmes cried in his last recorded words — August, 1914 — "You are the one fixed point in a changing age."

But Watson had much to suffer from Holmes before he heard that compliment. There was an explosion in *The Copper Beeches* about this matter of Watson's literary efforts.

" 'It seems to me I have done you full justice in the matter,' I remarked with some coldness, for I was repelled by the egotism which I had more than once observed to be a strong factor in my friend's singular character."

In *The Sign of Four* he had already had much to bear——

" 'You have attempted to tinge it with romanticism,' Holmes had said, referring to an earlier memoir, 'which produces much the same effect as if you had worked a love-story or an elopement into the fifth proposition of Euclid.'

"I was annoyed at this criticism of a work which had been specially designed to please him. I confess, too, that I was irritated by the egotism which seemed to demand that every line of my pamphlet should be devoted to his special doings."

Holmes once remarked: "Watson's reports are most incriminating documents"; but the final note in this minor discord was struck when Holmes took up the pen and wrote *The Blanched Soldier*.

"The ideas of my friend Watson, though limited, are extremely pertinacious. For a long time he has worried me to write an experience of my own. Perhaps I have rather invited this persecution, since I have often had occasion to point out to him how superficial are his own accounts and to accuse him of pandering to popular taste instead of confining himself rigidly to facts and figures.

" 'Try it yourself, Holmes,' he has retorted, and I am compelled to admit that, having taken my pen in hand, I do begin to realise that the matter must be presented in such a way as may interest the reader."

In dealing with femininity Watson, of course, was the tried and practised hand.

"In an experience of women which extends over many nations and three separate continents, I have never looked on a face that gave clearer promise of a refined and sensitive nature."

This refers to his future wife, and he further describes her as "a blonde young lady, small, dainty, well-gloved, and dressed in the most perfect taste." Holmes, being a misanthropist, was quite willing to encourage Watson in this pet conceit.

" 'Now, Watson, the fair sex is your department,' said Sherlock Holmes with a smile. 'You saw how she manoeuvred to have the light on her back.'

" 'Yes, she chose the one chair in the room.'

" 'And yet the motives of women are inscrutable. You remember the woman at Margate whom I suspected for the same cause? No powder on her nose — that proved to be the correct solution. How can you build on such a quicksand?' "

Some suspicion of Watson's ideas for the home will have been formed on realising that he was the kind of man who would be really pleased to see his wife's old school friends about the place; but he spares us nothing.

"As we drove away I stole a glance back and I still seem to see that little group on the step — the two graceful clinging figures, the half-opened door, the hall light shining through the stained glass, the barometer, and the bright stair rods. It was soothing to catch even that passing glimpse of a tranquil English home."

The appeal of the stained glass and the barometer must have been almost irresistible to Watson. And the reality of connubial bliss quite came up to his expectations——

"One night — it was June, '89 — there came a ring to my bell, about the hour when a man gives his first yawn and glances at the clock."

This is all the undiluted Watson, but we fail to trace any sign of the influence of Mrs. Watson in the menage. Writing of this time, he says——

"I had seen little of Holmes lately. My marriage had drifted us away from each other. My own complete happiness and the home-centered interests which rise up around a man who finds himself master of his own establishment were sufficient to absorb all my attention.

" 'Wedlock suits you,' Holmes noted too. 'I think, Watson, you have put on seven-and-a-half pounds since I saw you.' "

These are tributes to home and domesticity rather than to Mrs. Watson personally; Conan Doyle must take rank with Scott, Dickens, and many another, who have been incapable of drawing real live women. The slaying of Mrs. Watson is not a tragedy like Sinclair Lewis' cruel murder of Leora in *Martin Arrowsmith*, a murder which was all the more wanton because it was a purposeless crime, but when Mrs. Watson was so little alive her death cannot have made very much difference to her. It is for her life rather than for her death that one would lament. The tragedy of a wife whose home and happiness is wrecked by the drunkenness or gambling of her husband is well known, but the plight of a woman who pines at home while her always devoted and respectable husband goes out on the tiles at night with a six-shooter in his pocket, and in company with a man whose influence with him is stronger than her own, is forlorn indeed.

But at least one mark of Mrs. Watson remains. In *The Man with the Twisted Lip*, John (or James) H. Watson, M.D., utters the following astounding words: "A little blonde woman stood in the opening, clad in some sort of light *mousseline-de-soie*, with a touch of fluffy pink chiffon at her neck and wrists."

"Holmes looked at me thoughtfully and shook his head.

" 'I never get your limits, Watson,' he said. 'There are untold possibilities about you. Take a wire down, like a good fellow.' "

This is a later comment, but it applies. Mrs. Watson, her personality and her influence fade out of the picture, and Watson after the fleeting exhibition of individuality which the married state gave him,

Illustration: Sidney Paget 1890

becomes more and more the willing puppet of Holmes.

"'I am inclined to think,' said I.

"'I should do so,' Holmes remarked impatiently.

"I believe I am one of the most long-suffering of mortals, but I admit I was annoyed at the sardonic interruption.

"'Really, Holmes,' I said severely, 'you are a little trying at times.'"

Yet Holmes, to do the fellow justice, knew his Watson, and how far he could go with him.

"Speaking of my old friend and biographer," he says, in *The Blanched Soldier*, "I would take this opportunity to remark that if I burden myself with a companion on any of my various little enquiries, it is not done out of sentiment or caprice, but it is that Watson has some remarkable characteristics of his own, to which, in his modesty, he has given little attention amid exaggerated estimates of my own performances. A confederate who foresees your conclusions and course of action is always dangerous, but one to whom each development is a perpetual surprise, and to whom the future is a closed book, is indeed, an ideal helpmate."

One of the few checks he got appears in *The Valley of Fear*——

"'You have heard me speak of Professor Moriarty?'

"'The famous scientific criminal as famous among crooks as——'

"'My blushes, Watson,' Holmes murmured in a deprecating voice.

"'I was about to say, as unknown to the public.'

"'A touch!" cried Holmes. 'A distinct touch! You are developing an unexpected pawky humour, Watson, against which I must learn to guard myself.'"

Holmes's wit resembled that of judges and schoolmasters; it was tried when there was little chance of repartee: a person of whom his friend said, "I have not heard him laugh often, and it always boded ill for somebody," is better fitted for the company of bees on the Sussex Downs than for the worthy Doctor, who was really well quit of him. Poor old Watson! He had to make many sacrifices for Holmes, he had to give up wife and home, not to mention the bull pup, and what more can be required of any man? But one suspects that the thrills of the chase in the company of his hero, or the pleasant evenings spent lounging over the fire, with his pipe in his mouth, a decanter at his side, and his feet in some favourite slippers of which an helpmeet might disapprove, were greater rewards than home or kindred had in their power to bestow on him.

Villains: Professor Moriarty

BY WILLIAM VAUGHAN

It is somewhat difficult to decide upon a character in which are adequately displayed the qualities a person must possess in order to occupy the position of being a distinguished villain. First of all, villains may be divided into two classes — violent or brutal villains being assigned to one, intellectual or clever villains to the other; and obviously in the latter class the greatest villain will be found.

The villain who, in my opinion, is the greatest I have read of is Professor Moriarty, the person who brought the career of Sherlock Holmes, when in its zenith, to an abrupt and deplorable end. A character such as is depicted in the last of those fascinating "Memoirs" forms really a splendid end to an entrancing series of absorbing tales, the only fault of which is that this character might have been developed a little more, and have been the centre of other adventures.

Professor Moriarty was an extraordinary man, being naturally clever and with great faculties, and it was only to be expected that the education he received should have developed them and have qualified him for the highest position in whatever career he followed.

However, when we find in him hereditary tendencies to crime, the diabolicalness of which increased as his mental powers were unfolded and extended, he becomes an object capable of the most fearful transgressions of all that is right or lawful.

His career is indeed difficult to describe, since he was never the actor in the crimes he planned, but was the centre of numerous agencies, upon whom, if the crime were unravelled, the punishment was visited.

Until the investigations and marvellous powers of Sherlock Holmes were brought to bear upon

SIDNEY PAGET

Left: Professor Moriarty, Holmes' great adversary, as depicted by Sidney Paget in 1893. Above: The arch-villain in one of his many screen appearances as played by Gustav von Seyffertitz in "Moriarty" (1922). The dashingly handsome Holmes is none other than John Barrymore! Right: This picture of the Professor was drawn in 1902 by Walker Hodgson to accompany William Vaughan's article.

the matter, the existence of such a person as this professor was never thought of, which shows his genius.

He is compared to a spider in its web, the numerous quivers and vibrations of which are each known and understood by that insect: but a more appropriate comparison is, I think, formed in likening him to the brain of a man; like that he was unseen, unheard and, in fact, unknown, until the actions of the various parts of the body show that there must exist a central governing force, and in this force we find the greatest villain in fiction — Professor Moriarty.

Some personalia about Sherlock Holmes

BY ARTHUR CONAN DOYLE

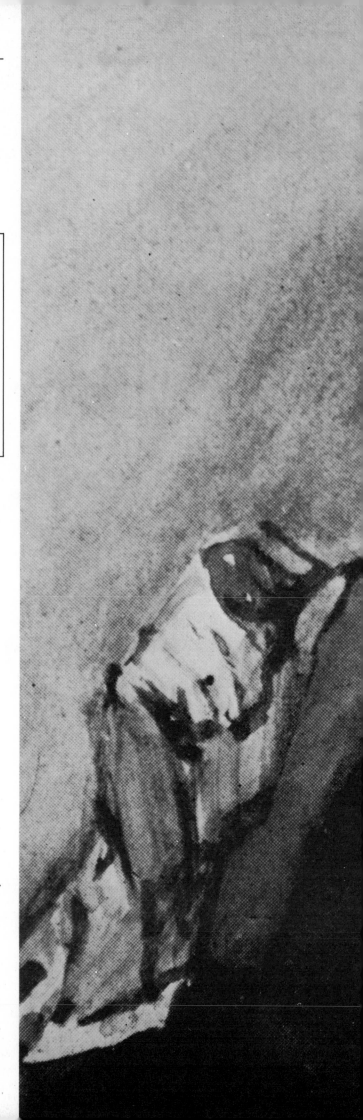

At the request of the Editor I have spent some days in looking over an old letter-box in which from time to time I have placed letters referring directly or indirectly to the notorious Mr. Holmes. I wish now that I had been more careful in preserving the references to this gentleman and his little problems. A great many have been lost or mislaid. His biographer has been fortunate enough to find readers in many lands, and the reading has elicited the same sort of response, though in many cases that response has been in a tongue difficult to comprehend. Very often my distant correspondent could neither spell my own name nor that of my imaginary hero, as in a good number of recent instances. Many such letters have been from Russians. Where the Russian letters have been in the vernacular I have been compelled, I am afraid, to take them as read, but when they have been in English they have been among the most curious in my collection. There was one young lady who began all her epistles with the words "Good Lord." Another had a large amount of guile underlying her simplicity. Writing from Warsaw she stated that she had been bedridden for two years, and that my novels had been her only, etc., etc. So touched was I by this flattering statement that I at once prepared an autographed parcel of them to complete the fair invalid's collection. By good luck, however, I met a brother author upon the same day to whom I recounted the touching incident. With a cynical smile he drew an identical letter out of his pocket. His novels also had been for two years her only, etc., etc. I do not know how many more the lady had written to, but if, as I imagine, her correspondence had extended to several countries, she must have amassed a rather interesting library.

The young Russian's habit of addressing me as "Good Lord" had an even stranger parallel at home, which links it up with the subject of this article.

23

Shortly after I received a knighthood I had a bill from a tradesman which was quite correct and businesslike in every detail save that it was made out to Sir Sherlock Holmes. I hope that I can stand a joke as well as my neighbours, but this particular piece of humour seemed rather misapplied, and I wrote sharply upon the subject. In response to my letter there arrived at my hotel a very repentant clerk, who expressed his sorrow at the incident, but kept on repeating the phrase, "I assure you, sir, that it was *bona fide.*" "What do you mean by *bona fide?*" I asked. "Well, sir, my mates in the shop told me that you had been

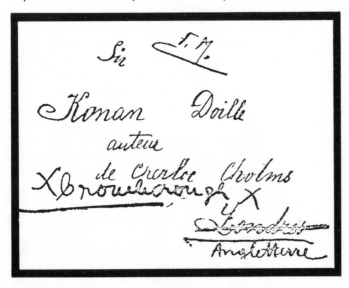

knighted, and that when a man was knighted he changed his name, and that you had taken that one." I need not say that my annoyance vanished, and that I laughed as heartily as his pals were probably doing round the corner.

There are certain problems which are continually recurring in these Sherlock Holmes letters. One of them has exercised men's minds in the most out-of-the-way places, from Labrador to Tibet; indeed, if a matter needs thought it is just the men in these outlying stations who have the time and solitude for it. I dare say I have had twenty letters upon the one point alone. It arises in "The Adventure of the Priory School," where Holmes, glancing at the track of a bicycle, says, "It is evidently going from us, not towards us." He did not give his reasoning, which my correspondents resent, and all assert that the deduction is impossible. As a matter of fact it is simple enough upon soft undulating ground such as the moor in question. The weight of the rider falls most upon the hind wheel, and in soft soil it makes a perceptibly deeper track. Where the machine goes up a slope this hind mark would be very much deeper; where it goes down a slope rapidly it would be hardly deeper at all. Thus the depth of the mark of the hind wheel would show which way the bike was travelling.

I never realized what an actual living personality Mr. Holmes was to many people until I heard the very pleasing story of the char-a-banc of French schoolboys on a tour to London, who, when asked what they wanted to see first, replied unanimously that they wanted to see Mr. Holmes's lodgings in Baker Street. Rather less pleasing, though flattering in their way, were the letters of abuse which showered upon me

when it was thought that I had killed him. "You brute!" was the promising opening of one lady's epistle. The most trenchant criticism of the stories as a series came from a Cornish boatman, who remarked to me: "When Mr. Holmes had that fall he may not have been killed, but he was certainly injured, for he was never the same man afterwards." I hope the allegation is not true — and, indeed, those who have read the stories backward, from the latest to the first, assure me that it is not so — but it was a shrewd thrust none the less.

One of the quaintest proofs of his reality to many people is that I have frequently received autograph books by post, asking me to procure his signature. When it was announced that he was retiring from practice and intended to keep bees on the South Downs I had several letters offering to help him in his project. Two of them lie before me as I write. One says: "Will Mr. Sherlock Holmes require a housekeeper for his country cottage at Christmas? I know someone who loves a quiet country life, and bees especially — an old-fashioned, quiet woman." The other, which is addressed to Holmes himself, says: "I see by some of the morning papers that you are about to retire and take up bee-keeping. If correct I shall be pleased to render you service by giving any advice you may require. I trust you will read this letter in the same spirit in which it is written, for I make this offer in return for many pleasant hours." Many other letters have reached me in which I have been implored to put my correspondents in touch with Mr. Holmes, in order that he might elucidate some point in their private affairs.

Occasionally I have been so far confused with my own character that I have been asked to take up professional work upon these lines. I had, I remember, one offer, in the case of an aristocratic murder trial in Poland some years ago, to go across and look into the matter upon my own terms. I need not say that I would not do such a thing for money, since I am diffident as to how far my own services would be of any value; but I have several times as an amateur been happy to have been of some assistance to people in distress. I can say, though I touch wood as I say it, that I have never entirely failed in any attempt which I have made to reduce Holmes's methods to practical use, save in one instance to which I allude later. For the case of Mr. Edalji I can claim little credit, for it did not take any elaborate deduction to come to the conclusion that a man who is practically blind did not make a journey at night which involved crossing a main line of railway, and would have tested a trained athlete had he been called upon to do it in the time. The man was obviously innocent, and it is a disgrace to this country that he has never received a penny of compensation for the three years which he spent in jail. A more complex case is that of Oscar Slater, who is still working out his sentence as a convict. I have examined the evidence carefully, including the supplementary evidence given at the very limited and unsatisfactory commission appointed to inquire into the matter, and I have not the faintest doubt that the man is innocent. When the judge asked him at the trial whether he had anything to say why the sentence of death for the murder of Miss Gilchrist should not be pronounced upon him, he cried aloud, "My Lord, I did not know there was such a woman in the world." I am convinced that this was the literal truth. However, it is proverbially impossible to prove a negative, so there the matter must stand until the people of Scotland insist upon a real investigation into all the circumstances which surround this deplorable case.

A few of the problems which have come my way have been very similar to some which I had invented for the exhibition of the reasoning of Mr. Holmes. I might perhaps quote one in which that gentleman's

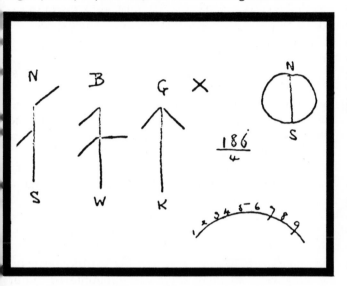

method of thought was copied with complete success. The case was as follows. A gentleman had disappeared. He had drawn a bank balance of forty pounds, which was known to be on him. It was feared that he had been murdered for the sake of the money. He had last been heard of stopping at a large hotel in London, having come from the country that day. In the evening he went to a music-hall performance, came out of it about ten o'clock, returned to his hotel, changed his evening clothes, which were found in his room next day, and disappeared utterly. No one saw him leave the hotel, but a man occupying a neighbouring room declared that he had heard him moving during the night. A week had elapsed at the time that I was consulted, but the police had discovered nothing. Where was the man?

These were the whole of the facts as communicated to me by his relatives in the country. Endeavouring to see the matter through the eyes of Mr. Holmes, I answered by return of post that he was evidently either in Glasgow or in Edinburgh. It proved later that he had as a fact gone to Edinburgh, though in the week that had passed he had moved to another part of Scotland.

There I should leave the matter, for, as Dr. Watson has often shown, a solution explained is a mystery spoiled. However, at this state the reader can lay down the book and show how simple it all is by working out the problem for himself. He has all the data which were ever given to me. For the sake of those, however, who have no turn for such conundrums I will try to indicate the links which make the chain. The one advantage which I possessed was that I was familiar with the routine of London hotels — though, I fancy, it differs little from that of hotels elsewhere.

The first thing was to look at the facts and separate what was certain from what was conjecture. It was *all* certain except the statement of the person who heard the missing man in the night. How could he tell such a sound from any other sound in a large hotel? That point could be disregarded if it traversed the general conclusions. The first clear deduction was that the man had meant to disappear. Why else should he draw all his money? He had got out of the hotel during the night. But there is a night-porter in all hotels, and it is impossible to get out without his knowledge when the door is once shut. The door is shut after the theatre-goers return — say at twelve o'clock. Therefore the man left the hotel before twelve o'clock. He had come from the music-hall at ten, had changed his clothes, and had departed with his bag. No one had seen him do so. The inference is that he had done it at the moment when the hall was full of the returning guests, which is from eleven to eleven-thirty. After that hour, even if the door were still open, there are few people coming and going; so that he with his bag would certainly have been seen.

Having got so far upon firm ground we now ask ourselves why a man who desires to hide himself should go out at such an hour. If he intended to conceal himself in London he need never have gone to the hotel at all. Clearly, then, he was going to catch a train which would carry him away. But a man who is deposited by a train in any provincial station during the night is likely to be noticed, and he might be sure that when the alarm was raised and his description given some guard or porter would remember him. Therefore his destination would be some large town, which he would reach in daylight hours, as a terminus, where all his fellow-passengers would disembark and where he would lose himself in the crowd. When one turns up the time-table and sees that the great Scotch expresses bound for Edinburgh and Glasgow start about midnight, the goal is reached. As for his dress-suit, the fact that he abandoned it proved that he intended to adopt a line of life where there were no social amenities. This deduction also proved to be correct.

I quote such a case in order to show that the general lines of reasoning advocated by Holmes have a real practical application to life. In another case where a girl had become engaged to a young foreigner who suddenly disappeared I was able by a similar process of deduction to show her very clearly both whither he had gone and how unworthy he was of her affections. On the other hand, these semi-scientific methods are occasionally laboured and slow as compared with the results of the rough-and-ready practical man. Lest I should seem to have been throwing bouquets either to myself or to Mr. Holmes, let me state that on the occasion of a burglary of the village inn, within a stone-throw of my house, the village constable, with no theories at all, had seized the culprit, while I had got no farther than that he was a left-handed man with nails in his boots.

The unusual or dramatic effects which lead to the invocation of Mr. Holmes in fiction are, of course, great aids to him in reaching a conclusion. It is the case where there is nothing to get hold of which is the deadly one. I heard of such a one in America which would certainly have presented a formidable problem. A gentleman of blameless life, starting off for a Sunday evening walk with his family, suddenly observed that he had forgotten his stick. He went back into the house, the door of which was still open, and he left his people waiting for him outside. He never reappeared, and from that day to this there has been no clue as to what befell him. This was certainly one of the strangest cases of which I have ever heard in real life.

Another very singular case came within my own observation. It was sent to me by an eminent London publisher. This gentleman had in his employment a head of department whose name we shall take as Musgrave. He was a hard-working person with no special feature in his character. Mr. Musgrave died, and several years after his death a letter was received addressed to him, care of his employers. It bore the postmark of a tourist resort in the West of Canada, and had the note "Conf[1] films" upon the outside of the envelope, with the words "Report Sy" in one corner. The publishers naturally opened the envelope, as they had no note of the dead man's relatives. Inside were two blank sheets of paper. The letter, I may add, was registered. The publisher, being unable to make anything of this, sent it on to me, and I submitted the blank sheets to every possible chemical and heat test, with no result whatever. Beyond the fact that the writing appeared to be that of a woman, there is nothing to add to this account. The matter was, and remains, an insoluble mystery. How the correspondent could have something so secret to say to Mr. Musgrave and yet not be aware that this person had been dead for several years is very hard to understand — or why blank sheets should be so carefully registered through the post. I may add that I did not trust the sheets to my own chemical tests, but had the best expert advice, without getting any result. Considered as a case it was a failure — and a very tantalizing one.

Mr. Sherlock Holmes has always been a fair mark for practical jokers, and I have had numerous bogus cases of various degrees of ingenuity, marked cards, mysterious warnings, cipher messages, and other curious communications. Upon one occasion, as I was entering the hall to take part in an amateur billiard competition, I was handed a small packet which had been left for me. Upon opening it I found a piece of ordinary green chalk such as is used in billiards. I was amused by the incident, and I put the chalk into my waistcoat pocket and used it during the game. Afterwards I continued to use it until one day, some months later, as I rubbed the tip of my cue, the face of the chalk crumpled in, and I found it was hollow. From the recess thus exposed I drew out a small slip of paper with the words, "From Arsene Lupin to Sherlock Holmes." Imagine the state of mind of the joker who took such trouble to accomplish such a result!

One of the mysteries submitted to Mr. Holmes was rather upon the psychic plane, and therefore beyond his powers. The facts as alleged are most remarkable, though I have no proof of their truth save that the lady wrote earnestly and gave both her name and address. The person, whom we will call Mrs. Seagrave, had been given a curious second-hand ring, snake-shaped, and of dull gold. This she took from her finger at night. One night she slept in it, and had a fearsome dream in which she seemed to be pushing off some furious creature which fastened its teeth into her arm. On awakening the pain in the arm continued, and next day the imprint of a double set of teeth appeared upon the arm, with one tooth of the lower jaw missing. The marks were in the shape of blue-black bruises which had not broken the skin. "I do not know," says my correspondent, "what made me think the ring had anything to do with the matter, but I took a dislike to the thing and did not wear it for some months, when, being on a visit, I took to wearing it again." To make a long story short, the same thing happened, and the lady settled the matter for ever by dropping her ring into the hottest corner of the kitchen-range. This curious story, which I believe to be genuine, may not be as supernatural as it seems. It is well known that in some subjects a strong mental impression does produce a physical effect. Thus a very vivid nightmare-dream with the impression of a bite might conceivably produce the mark of a bite. Such cases are well attested in medical annals. The second incident would, of course, arise by unconscious suggestion from the first. None the less, it is a very interesting little problem, whether psychic or material.

Buried treasures are naturally among the problems which have come to Mr. Holmes. One genuine case was accompanied by the diagram here reproduced. It refers to an Indiaman which was wrecked upon the South African coast in the year 1782. If I were a younger man I should be seriously inclined to go personally and look into that matter. The ship contained a remarkable treasure, including, I believe, the old crown regalia of Delhi. It is surmised that they buried these near the coast and that this chart is a note of the spot. Each Indiaman in those days had its own semaphore code, and it is conjectured that the three marks upon the left are signals from a three-armed semaphore. Some record of their meaning might perhaps even now be found in the old papers of the India Office. The circle upon the right gives the compass bearings. The larger semicircle may be the curved edge of a reef or of a rock. The figures above are the indications how to reach the X which marks the treasure. Possibly they may give the bearings as 186 feet from the 4 upon the semicircle. The scene of the wreck is a lonely part of the country, but I shall be surprised if sooner or later someone does not seriously set to work to solve the mystery.

One last word before I close these jottings about my imaginary character. It is not given to every man to see the child of his brain endowed with life through the genius of a great sympathetic artist, but that was my good fortune when Mr. Gillette turned his mind and his great talents to putting Holmes upon the stage. I cannot end my remarks more fittingly than by my thanks to the man who changed a creature of thin air into an absolutely convincing human being.

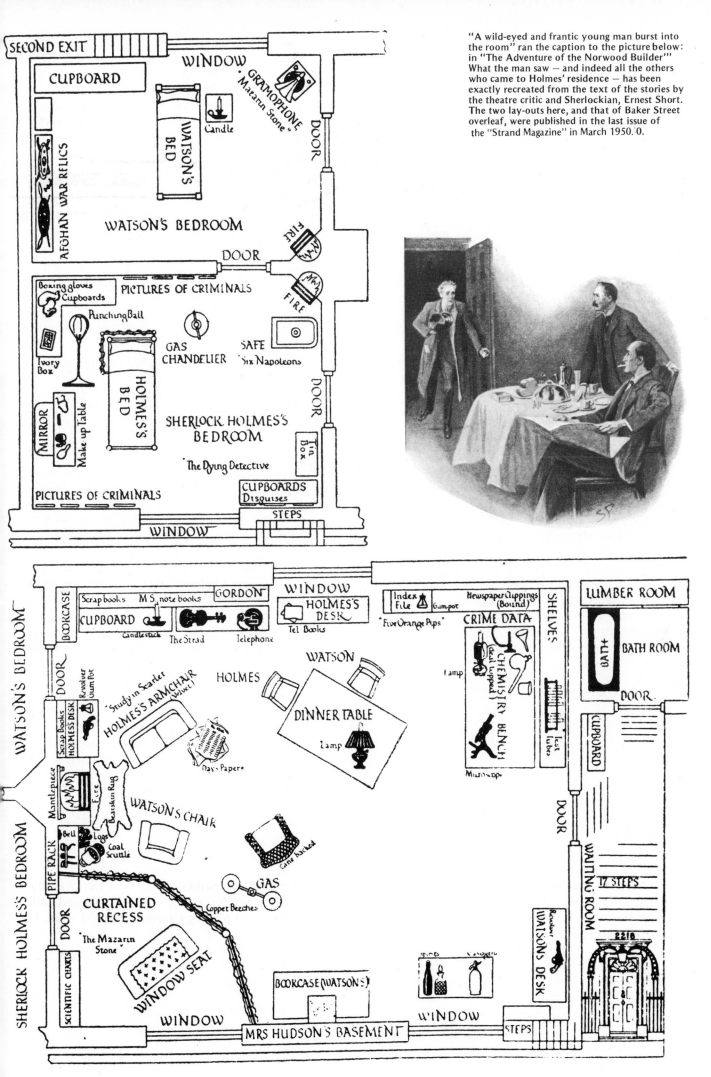

SECOND EXIT

CUPBOARD

WINDOW

GRAMOPHONE "Mazarin Stone"

Candle

DOOR

WATSON'S BED

AFGHAN WAR RELICS

WATSON'S BEDROOM

FIRE

DOOR

FIRE

Boxing gloves Cupboards

PICTURES OF CRIMINALS

Punching Ball

GAS CHANDELIER

SAFE "Six Napoleons"

Ivory Box

HOLMES'S BED

MIRROR

Make up Table

SHERLOCK HOLMES'S BEDROOM

Tin Box

DOOR

"The Dying Detective"

PICTURES OF CRIMINALS

CUPBOARDS Disguises

STEPS

WINDOW

"A wild-eyed and frantic young man burst into the room" ran the caption to the picture below: in "The Adventure of the Norwood Builder'" What the man saw — and indeed all the others who came to Holmes' residence — has been exactly recreated from the text of the stories by the theatre critic and Sherlockian, Ernest Short. The two lay-outs here, and that of Baker Street overleaf, were published in the last issue of the "Strand Magazine" in March 1950.'0.

WATSON'S BEDROOM

BOOKCASE

Scrap books   M S. note books   GORDON

CUPBOARD

Candlestick   The Strad   Telephone

WINDOW

HOLMES'S DESK

Tel Books

Index File   Gum pot

"Five Orange Pips"

Newspaper Clippings (Bound)

SHELVES

LUMBER ROOM

BATH ROOM

CRIME DATA

CHEMISTRY BENCH

DOOR

Lamp

Test tubes

DOOR

CUPBOARD

Scrap books   HOLMES'S DESK   Revolver Gum Pot

DOOR

"Study in Scarlet"

HOLMES'S ARMCHAIR (Velvet)

HOLMES

WATSON

DINNER TABLE

Lamp

Days Papers

Microscope

Mantelpiece   Fire   Bearskin Rug

WATSON'S CHAIR

Cane backed

WAITING ROOM

Bell   Logs   Coal Scuttle

PIPE RACK

17 STEPS

GAS

DOOR

CURTAINED RECESS

Copper Beeches

WATSON'S DESK

Revolver

"The Mazarin Stone"

SHERLOCK HOLMES'S BEDROOM

SCIENTIFIC CHARTS

WINDOW SEAT

BOOKCASE (WATSON'S)

221B

WINDOW

WINDOW

STEPS

MRS HUDSON'S BASEMENT

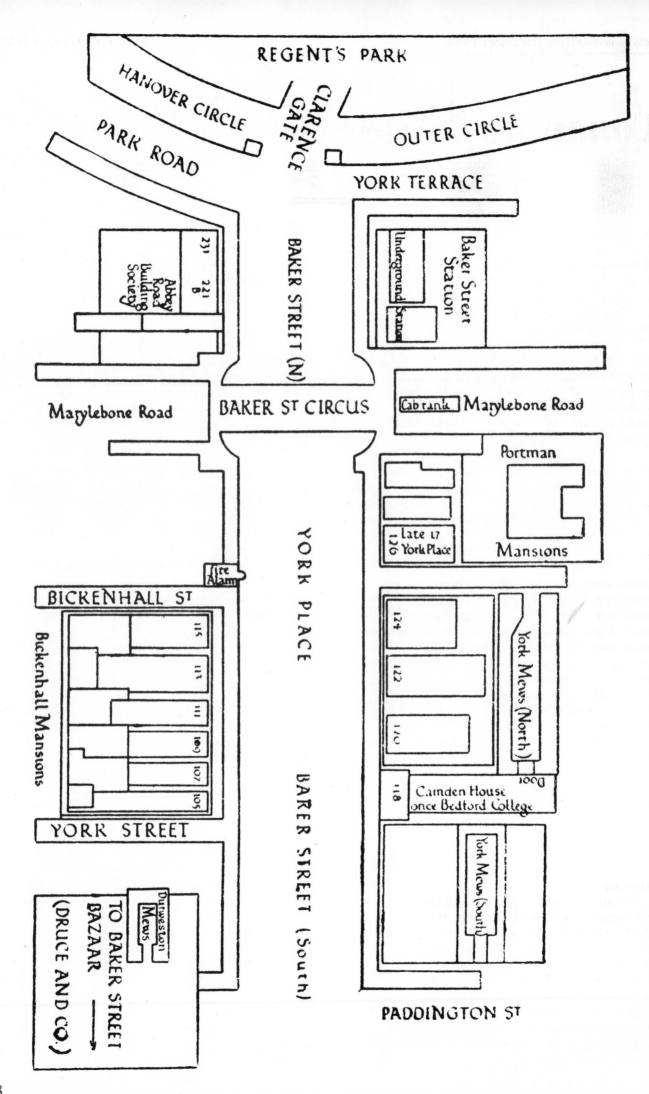

Pearsons Magazine December 1934   BY LADY CONAN DOYLE

Conan Doyle was Sherlock Holmes

My husband was so versatile in his literary work that it is difficult in a short space to describe the various sides of his genius, and it would take many pages to tell at all adequately of his remarkably noble and wonderful character — each facet so striking that whoever came near him at once sensed the inner greatness both of his soul and mind.

He never believed in shoddy work, but was intensely thorough in anything he undertook. He told me that before he began to write "The White Company" (his favourite book of all he ever wrote) he read over sixty books all dealing with that period — books on heraldry, falconry, armour, etc. He absorbed so much knowledge of those days that he might actually have lived in them, so true an atmosphere, so living a spirit did he create in his romantic and finely-coloured story "The White Company" — a virile, living tale of those days.

My husband trained himself to write when the flow of inspiration came, anywhere and in any circumstances. He had that rare faculty of being able entirely to isolate his mind, as it were, from his surroundings. He had no settled hours for work. Sometimes he would be in the study before the servants were up, or he would go in and write after a game of golf. He would never force the work. He only wrote when the inspiration was upon him, and when it just flowed from his pen, so that he could hardly set it down quickly enough. He was a tremendously hard worker. The following must surely be a record. He wrote and produced his play *The Speckled Band* in three weeks, as well as dealing with an enormous correspondence and many other matters during the time!

He sometimes wrote his Sherlock Holmes stories in a room full of people talking! He would write in a train with the hum of conversation around him, or in a cricket pavilion during the match, while waiting for the rain to stop.

He used to feel that Sherlock Holmes tended to obscure his other higher literary works, such as his historical novels.

He had that rare gift of making a character so real and human and so living a personality. Think of Challenger, that great, gruff, lovable character with his super-brain. Then the conceited but delightful Brigadier Gerard; Sir Nigel, the chivalrous, adventurous knight, the embodiment of all that is splendid in a man; Sherlock Holmes with his rapier-like brain.

He loved building up his fictional characters with all their little idiosyncrasies, their strengths and weaknesses, so that they became like living personalities to him, and that is why, in the minds of so many of his readers also, they are like familiar friends.

I have sometimes felt that one of the reasons why he was able to make his characters so very real was that he was able to imbue them, all unknown to himself, with parts of his own character and personality.

Take, for instance, Sherlock Holmes and my husband's own extraordinary powers of deduction and analysis! The public does not realise that my husband had the Sherlock Holmes brain, and that sometimes he privately solved mysteries that had non-plussed the police. He was able, through his remarkable powers of deduction and inference, to locate missing people whose relatives had given them up as lost or murdered.

My husband often used the Sherlock Holmes line of deduction in a most interesting way in determining the profession or circumstances of people whom he observed in public. On every occasion when the opportunity arose, and we checked up with his theories, we invariably found them to be correct.

Take, again, one of his other creations, Challenger, that splendid brave scientist who had the courage of his opinions, and who was in knowledge ahead of his time, as my husband was in his psychic knowledge. Then Sir Nigel, that most chivalrous old knight — no knight of old was more full of the most perfect chivalry and nobility of character than my husband, and a wife knows better than all others the true character of a man. Rodney Stone portrays the spirit of clean, fearless English sport. My husband was full of it, and sport in all directions was his great relaxation from the responsibilities of life. Also the humorous Brigadier Gerard — my husband's sense of humour was boyish as well as fine and scintillating.

His booklet "The Boer War, Its Cause and Conduct," changed the antagonistic attitude of nations against us into a clearer understanding of the justice of England's cause. In the composition of his monumental work — "The History of the Great War," his great spirit laboured against every conceivable difficulty in obtaining correct information regarding the part played by the British Army, in order that he might hand down a record to posterity of the magnificent bravery and sacrifice made by the men of the Empire. The writing of the "History of the Boer War," and the colossal task that he undertook in writing his "History of the Great War," reflected the patriotic soul of my husband and his intense love of his country. That same spirit of his shows itself in the characters of the tenacious fighters depicted in his historical novels.

As to my companion neither the country nor the sea presented the slightest attraction to him. He loved to lie in the very centre of five millions of people with his filaments stretching out and running through them, responsive to every little rumour or suspicion of unsolved crime.

Yours sincerely
A Conan Doyle.

It was his deep sense of justice which made him take up the cudgels so indefatigably on behalf of Edalji and Slater, in which he was instrumental in reversing two serious miscarriages of justice. At all times he was a fearless fighter on behalf of the oppressed and the victims of injustice.

His style was wonderful in its simplicity — with never a redundant word — surely the highest form of art. People should write as they talk. An involved style is not indicative of a profound mind, but rather of a confused one.

Like all truly great men, my husband was innately modest. I never heard a conceited word pass his lips; he was also utterly without jealousy, and he loved to hear of the success of others, and was the first to give his praise and encouragement. He had great sympathy for the struggles of young writers and did all he could to help them. He used his genius to its highest in every direction. In all his many and numerous writings on varied subjects there is not one word which could leave the tiniest smudge upon the mind or soul of any reader, and the ideals and spirit of honesty, chivalry, nobility and human loveliness running through his books could only leave a subconscious desire in the minds of the readers to be a better man or woman.

Left: Arthur Conan Doyle at his desk with a specimen of his signature and an extract in his own handwriting from the manuscript of one of the stories. **Below:** Doyle was a keen sportsman among his many interests and is shown here about to set off for a ride with his wife.

The Sunday Times June 10 1934

SHERLOCK HOLMES SAGA: HIS "PRIVATE LIFE"

The Private Life of Sherlock Holmes by Vincent Starrett (Ivor Nicholson and Watson.)

BY J. M. BULLOCH

When, after trying to fill up his time and his empty purse by writing magazine stories, Dr. Arthur Conan Doyle produced "A Study in Scarlet," he had not the slightest idea that he was creating one of the great figures of fiction. Indeed, half a dozen publishers turned it down, and when at last Ward Lock offered him £25 for it, lock, stock, and barrel for "Beeton's Christmas Annual" in 1887, he took the fee without hesitation, for he had to live. To-day that copy of the annual is a collector's prize.

What Mr. Starrett, a devoted (Chicago) disciple, who has been writing on the subject for nearly 20 years, has done is to compile a rough-and-ready guide to the Sherlockian saga. It is not a very satisfactory book, for it appears to fall between two stools; it is not quite explanatory enough for the beginner, or advanced enough for the expert.

Literary detection

It may, however, tempt the former to play the detective for himself. Thus, though Mr. Starrett inventories 90 miscellaneous items about Sherlock Holmes, he remarks that the list does not attempt to include "one-hundredth part" of the many books, pamphlets, articles, burlesques, and other writings about him. Similarly, in the bibliography of the editions of Sherlock Holmes himself, a rough attempt might have been made to enumerate translations into foreign languages.

Certainly, more might have been given about Dr. Joseph Bell (1837-1911), the prototype of Sherlock, all the more as, strange to say, he is not in such books of reference as the Dictionary of National Biography and the popular encyclopaedias. Mr. Starrett has no doubt that "the real Holmes was Conan Doyle himself." He scores a point when he says:—

'In innumerable ways throughout his life of extraordinary service, the British novelist demonstrated the truth of the assertion. From first to last — as student, physician, writer, spiritualist, and prophet of war — he was always the private detective, the seeker after hidden truth, the fathomer of obscure mysteries, the hound of justice upon the trail of injustice and official apathy.'

Conan Doyle's indifference

Sir Arthur's indifference to his detective displayed itself when William Gillette, who made a fortune by dramatising the stories in an "absurd and preposterous melodrama," wired him, "May I marry Holmes?" Doyle, then immensely preoccupied with the South African war, wired back, "You may marry or murder him or do what you like with him." Amid the olla — podrida of curious facts collected by Mr. Starrett, we are reminded that Professor Moriarty, who gets the name of Robert in the play and nowhere else, was modelled on Adam Worth, who stole the Gainsborough Duchess in 1876.

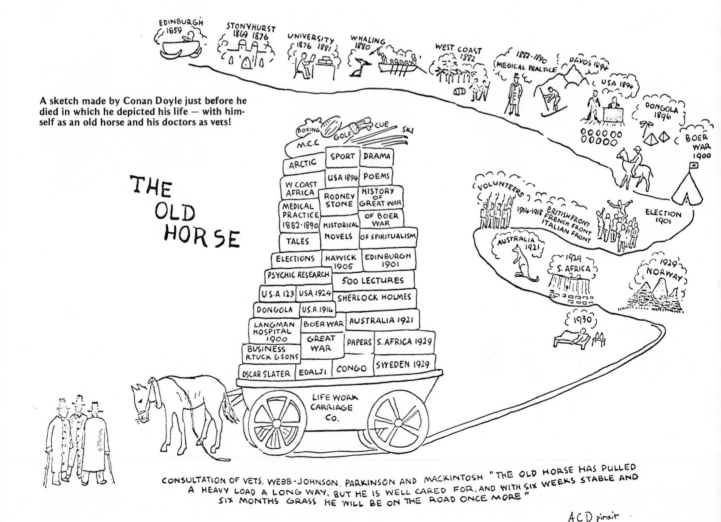

A sketch made by Conan Doyle just before he died in which he depicted his life — with himself as an old horse and his doctors as vets!

The Bookman August 1932   BY EDMUND PEARSON

Holmes among the illustrators

Conan Doyle imagined Sherlock Holmes as a man with a thin hawk-like nose, piercing eyes, and so excessively lean that he seemed even taller than his actual six feet. Thus the author described him in the first Holmes story. *A Study in Scarlet.*

Later, Doyle emphasized his idea that Holmes had a "razor-like face; a great hawk's-bill of a nose; two small eyes set close together" and that he was powerful but ugly. His first important illustrator, Sidney Paget, made a Holmes who was tall, but not extremely tall, and who was far from "ugly". Dr. Doyle thought that this was because Paget had used his brother Walter as a model. He believed that the more comely detective was perhaps fortunately drawn to please the ladies. The writer of the sketch of Paget in the *Dictionary of National Biography*, however, denies that the artist used his brother or anyone else as a model. He leaves you to suppose that Paget drew Holmes from his own fancy, based on Doyle's description as given in the stories comprised in the *Adventures.*

One or two artists preceded Paget. Sherlock Holmes appeared for the first time in print in 1887, when *A Study in Scarlet* was published in that queer-looking periodical, *Beeton's Christmas Annual.* Despite many excellencies, and one surprise never bettered in any of the tales, this novel attracted little notice. For the initial appearance of a detective whose exploits were to be recorded for nearly forty years, a veteran illustrator of that day, D. H. Friston, was called upon.

This first picture of Holmes would distress the devotees. Friston's Sherlock is neither handsome nor intellectual; he wears undertaker's side-whiskers, an ulster with a cape, and a hat like nothing on sea or land — a sort of bastard child of a bowler out of a sombrero. With a magnifying glass as big as a sunflower, he is examining the word *RACHE* written in blood upon the wall. About him, in grotesque attitudes, stand Watson — with a walrus's moustache — and the Scotland Yarders, Gregson and Lestrade. Mr. Friston seems to have thought that the scene was macabre, and that the characters should look like gargoyles.

In the second edition of the story, in book form, there are said to be six illustrations by the novelist's father, Charles Doyle. They should be interesting; Conan Doyle thought his father the greatest and most original of a family of artists.

The next Holmes story, another short novel, *The Sign of the Four*, appeared in *Lippincott's Magazine*, February, 1890. There is one illustration, a scene in India, in which Holmes does not appear.

Ten short stories which carried Holmes's fame

Holmes and Watson in Regent Street — one of the most famous of Sidney Paget's illustrations for "The Hound of the Baskervilles" (1901).

around the world, the *Adventures*, began in the *Strand Magazine*, July, 1891. For these the already mentioned Sidney Edward Paget, a young illustrator of about thirty, began to draw the Holmes whose features became familiar throughout the British Empire and to some early enthusiasts in the United States. His Holmes had a long nose, high forehead, rather bald temples, and, when at home in Baker Street, usually wore a frock coat.

One of the actors who impersonated Holmes in our own time — Arthur Wontner, in the screen play, *Sherlock Holmes's Fatal Hour* — closely resembled the detective of Paget's pictures.

There is an impression that Mr. William Gillette, in his play, first put Holmes in a deer-stalker's cap with visors fore and aft. In one of the early *Strand* stories, however, *The Boscombe Valley Mystery*, Dr. Doyle says that Holmes wore a "close-fitting cloth cap", and Paget shows him with a fore-and-after. Watson, even in

A youthful Holmes and Watson by W.H. Hyde for "The Yellow
Face" in "Harper's Weekly", 1895.

the country, sticks to his bowler. Mr. Gillette played Holmes in one of these caps, on one evening in London when he was headed for the Stepney gas chamber and rough work.

American editors, in 1893, began to be interested in Holmes, and the second series, the *Memoirs,* ran in *Harper's Weekly,* in addition to their English publication in the *Strand.* The American artist, Mr. W. H. Hyde, adorned the stories in *Harper's* with some striking pictures, but preferred to draw the actors in the criminal events rather than Holmes and Watson. The detective seldom appears, and when he does he is Mr. Hyde's own conception. One recognizes with difficulty, in this youth of the nineties with his short, light overcoat, either the cocaine addict of Baker Street or the expert boxer who twice knocked down Joseph Harrison, the thief of the Naval Treaty.

The *Memoirs* closed with *The Final Problem* and the "death" of Sherlock Holmes, who went over the cliffs of the Reichenbach, along with his enemy, Professor Moriarty. Nevertheless, in the autumn of 1901, the *Strand* began publication of the serial, *The Hound of the Baskervilles,* with Mr. Paget again illustrating the text. Dr. Doyle wisely made no reference to the fact that for six or seven years we had supposed Holmes to be lying on the Alpine mountains cold, but went on with his hero as if nothing had happened. The novel ran in both the English and American editions of the *Strand* — the American always one instalment behind the English. This caused one reader, who began the serial in London and carried on in this country, the agonizing experience of waiting *two* months for the next instalment, after perusing the blood-curdling words: "Mr. Holmes, they were the footprints of a gigantic hound!"

During the progress of this novel, and while everyone was guessing at its plot, THE BOOKMAN published some ingenious solutions contributed by excited readers, of whom I was one. They were all far astray. Mr. Arthur Bartlett Maurice told me that they were read by Dr. Doyle, who intimated that they were worthy of Gregson and Lestrade.

In this story, Paget presented Holmes and Watson in their best-tailored moments. Look at them in their glossy toppers, hot on the trail of the mysterious man in the hansom cab. The people, the omnibus, and the background of the Quadrant of Regent Street make it redolent of London, and full of the spirit of these tales.

Two years later, in 1903, Holmes's loyal followers were given satisfaction with a full explanation of his supposed death, and an account of where he had been and what he had been doing. On both sides of the ocean he re-appeared in the series called *The Return of Sherlock Holmes,* and in America, in *Collier's Weekly,* with the most interesting decorations of all time. Old Sherlockians will always be fond of the Paget drawings, but they must admit that the pictures made for this new series, by Frederic Dorr Steele, were not only satisfactory as portraits, but extremely attractive in detail.

The features of Holmes as drawn by Mr. Steele were clearly done under the William Gillette influence. Since 1899 Mr. Gillette had been playing Holmes, and to

thousands of playgoers he had become the perfect embodiment of the detective. They had never seen any other representation, and could not imagine one. The Steele pictures had in their turn an influence on the stage, or upon the screen, for it seems probable that the enormous number of properties assembled for the Baker Street scene in John Barrymore's film play (1922) originated in Mr. Steele's fascinating pictures of Holmes's rooms and their accessories. Mr. Steele was the first illustrator to suggest that Dr. Watson was a simple Simon: he gave the Doctor an extremely blonde moustache, and a good-natured face which verges on silliness.

It was Mr. Arthur I. Keller, in the American edition of *The Valley of Fear* (1915), who dealt the cruelest blow at Watson. From merely the innocent Johnny of Mr. Steele's drawings, Watson emerges in Mr. Keller's picture as *boobus Britannicus. The Valley of Fear* had

Above: The most famous American illustrator of the adventures, Frederic Dorr Steele, shows Holmes arresting Colonel Moran in "The Adventure of the Empty House", "Collier's Magazine", 1903.
Below: One of six pictures executed by Conan Doyle's father, Charles Doyle, for "A Study In Scarlet" in 1888. Note the bearded Holmes!

Left: Holmes and Inspector Lestrade arresting Jefferson Hope in George Hutchinson's illustration for the Ward Lock edition of "A Study In Scarlet" (1891). Centre: Charles R. Macauley's Holmes from "The Return of Sherlock Holmes" published by McClure, Phillips & Co. in 1905. Right: The much criticised Holmes and Watson picture by Arthur I. Keller for the "American Associated Saturday Magazine's" "The Valley of Fear" in 1914.

been illustrated in the *Strand* by Frank Wiles; it is a story of the Molly Maguires in Pennsylvania, and is one of the lesser items of Sherlockiana.

When the stories in *The Return* were published as a book in America, Mr. C. R. Macauley drew a few pictures of Holmes. One of these, a curiously feathery person, with some resemblance to William Gillette, is reproduced here.

Paget continued his pictures in the *Strand* until his death in 1908; four or five different artists followed him in his work on the Holmes stories, which went on, often at long intervals, for about seventeen years more. H. M. Brock is probably the best known of these illustrators, although he seems to have worked on one story only. The last of the *Strand* illustrators was Howard Elcock, who drew some vigorous pictures. He followed the Paget tradition as to Holmes's face. Altogether, even in this incomplete record, I have found the names of fifteen artists who have drawn Sherlock Holmes.

The stories afterwards collected in *His Last Bow* (1917) and *The Case Book of Sherlock Holmes* (1927) came out in various periodicals, illustrated by different artists. "It is with a heavy heart", as Dr. Watson said in beginning *The Final Problem*, that I record my opinion that in these stories the old fire was flickering; although, as in *The Bruce-Partington Plans*, it sometimes blazed up with the warmth of the early days.

It was chiefly in the stories contained in *The Case Book* that Dr. Doyle made the contradictory statements, and committed himself to the anachronisms about his two heroes, which have given Father Ronald Knox, Mr. S. C. Roberts, and other serio-comic investigators the basis for their amusing monographs on the early life of Dr. Watson, his mysterious second marriage, and other esoteric matters.

Mentioning William Gillette's early appearance on the stage as Holmes (revived in 1929) recalls that, in England, H. A. Saintsbury played Sherlock over 1400 times. Other English actors, chiefly in the cinema, who have impersonated Holmes include Eille Norwood, whose *Hound of the Baskervilles* was given here in 1922; Clive Brook; Arthur Wontner, whose screen play was one of the best; Raymond Massey; and Dennis Neilson-Terry. Mr. Massey brought Holmes up-to-date and gave him an office with stenographers, dictaphones, radio, and typewriters. This was much like showing Washington crossing the Delaware in an airplane — very pleasing to those who love to shatter tradition into bits.

John Barrymore's film (1922) was based on the Gillette stage play and had a remarkable cast which included Roland Young as Dr. Watson; Gustav von Seyffertitz as Professor Moriarty; William Powell as Forman Wells; and Louis Wolheim as Craigin.

Recalling these pictorial representations of the lean detective brings back happy memories, and makes the ancient Sherlockian murmur, in the words of Old English: "Great Days! Great Days!"

Once more Holmes and Watson sit by the fire in the rooms of that patient landlady: Mrs. Hudson. Once more the dense yellow fog swirls around the window panes, until Holmes chafes at his enforced inactivity. Then Mrs. Hudson is heard toiling up the stairs; she taps on the door, to announce — what mysterious personage? The King of Bohemia, in his black mask? Mr. Jabez Wilson, with his red hair and his curious story? Brother Mycroft, puffing and wheezing, to say that the Prime Minister is quite agitated, and that Sherlock must come at once? Or some beautiful and distressed lady, to tell of an unexplained and terrible death at midnight? Perhaps this time they are really going to find out what in Heaven's name *were* the Singular Adventures of the Grice Paterson in the Island of Uffa!

Anyhow, they will soon be in a hansom together; Watson with his old service revolver in his pocket, and the thrill of adventure in his heart.

Great Days! Great Days!

A NEW ADVENTURE OF
SHERLOCK HOLMES

For
CHRISTMAS
PRESENTS.
Nothing
Better
than
FRY'S
Chocolates
In Fancy Boxes.
See Page 34.

SOUTHAMPTON STREET

THE STRAND MAGAZINE

GRAND CHRISTMAS DOUBLE NUMBER

Geo: Newnes Ltd.

OFFICES

DEC. 1913

1/-

BY DESMOND MacCARTHY

The world of books: Sherlockismus!

"Sherlock Holmes and Dr. Watson." By H.W. Bell. (Constable.)
"Sherlock Holmes." By Thomas Blakeney. (Murray.)

In no department of research have so many high reputations been lost and won as in Sherlockology, The fierce light of investigation which has been directed upon No. 221B, Baker Street, during the present century, and upon the lives of the two friends inhabiting it, has revealed problems nigh insoluable, and of such intricacy as earlier readers of Dr. Watson's annals, even the most assiduous of them, never dreamt of. The state of Watsonian scholarship today, when compared with that of ten years ago is — it must be admitted — bewildering to laymen. The investigations of Knox, of Roberts, of "Evoe," and of others whose names are less widely known, though hardly less respected, of Vernon Rendall, Behrens of Corpus Christi College, Cambridge, Alan Parsons, A. A. Milne (whose plays and verses are unknown in the world where he won his real laurels) have unfortunately raised almost as many questions as they have laid to rest.

The chronology of the incidents recorded in the various books which constitute the canon from "The Study in Scarlet" onwards, is at many points still as doubtful as the order of some of Shakespeare's plays. Moreover, the misguided acumen of Knox has even thrown doubt upon the authenticity of the latter books of the canon itself. In "The Case Book" and "His Last Bow" he professed to have seen evidences of the hand of a deutero- and — possibly — of a trito-Watson. Whether in doing so he only yielded to those fickle humours which sometimes prompt men to literary frolics on the gravest subjects, or whether we must impute to him those rankling jealousies and that restless vanity which, alas, scholars of the brightest intelligence have been known to indulge, I leave others to decide.

A temperate reproof

Lack of space prevents me here from grappling with Knox and giving him a fall, and, for my part, I will never assert where I cannot persuade. Let it suffice to say that such conclusions could have only been reached by one deliberately bent on upsetting the tranquillity of the public mind, and by employing to that end a powerful intellect polluted by prejudice or a wayward temperament which naturally delights in giving an air of importance to trifles. Let me quote the concluding words of Roberts' rare pamphlet: "Note on

the Watson Problem" (Cambridge University Press, 1929); they carry reproof not less formidable for being temperate in expression: "Trifles such as these (he writes of 'Studies in the Literature of Sherlock Holmes') may be of some interest to the amateur of apocrypha, but it is to be hoped that serious students will rather devote their energies to the elucidation of the major problems of Watsonian chronology, the complexity of which we have sought but to adumbrate . . ." There speaks the true scholar; clear, simple, manly, rational, striking conviction in every word, unlike the refined and fantastic nonsense of one who, while pretending to be a friend to free-inquiry, would lead us into the pathless wilds of conjecture and keep us suspended over the bottomless gulfs of critical scepticism.

The above books compared

To tamper with the canon is only to sow strife among scholars and scatter the seeds of discord (though I hesitate to say it) with wanton irresponsibility. Let us face "the major problems" — heaven knows they bristle with difficulties! — together. They can only yield to collaboration and mutual help. It is in this spirit that we welcome the work of extraordinarily patient and minute research which stands first of the books mentioned at the head of this column. Mr. H. W. Bell's "Sherlock Holmes and Dr. Watson" leads us straight to the heart of these difficulties; while that of Mr. Thomas Blakeney, though admirably sound as a whole, is comparatively elementary. It is calculated to whet the appetite of the public — if such encouragement is necessary -- for further investigation, and it might very properly be placed in the hands of a lad on leaving school who knows his texts well, but whose studies have halted at the figure of the great detective himself, and is as yet unaware of the deeper significance and interest of Watson. Compared with Mr. H. W. Bell's book it is not an important contribution to what the Germans denominate *"Watsonischechronologieprobleme."* Yet, on the whole, it is the work of a more balanced judgment; though where the young reader is concerned I must enter one *caveat* with regard to it.

The general review of the character, opinions and habits of Sherlock Holmes is painstaking and complete; and high praise must be accorded to Mr. Blakeney for the thorough way in which he has given his references for every statement in it. But (and here comes what the Americans call the knock of regret) he has inclined to an error too common in such surveys, namely, that of supposing that the characteristics which were so marked in Sherlock Holmes in 1881, when first he shared "diggings" with his friend, necessarily persisted. We have evidence that age and success considerably tempered the Bohemianism of Holmes's habits, while long association with the commonplace culture of Watson inevitably widened his interests. The surprising list of the lacunae in his education given us in "A Study in Scarlet" does not apply to the later Holmes, as is shown by his constant if never striking references to literature. I will not go so far as to say that Mr. Blakeney ignores this obvious truth, but I wish to caution the beginner against the tendency to present Sherlock Holmes as a static character even more noticeable in other scholars.

The finances of Baker Street

And there is another point. In a popular but thorough book of this description, in my opinion the finances of Baker Street should have received more systematic attention. For such treatment the student can be referred to Behrens's privately circulated monograph. As everyone knows, it was economy that first compelled the two men to keep house together. Watson, with what may be called his superb normality, had found it impossible to live independently on his military pension of £209. 6s. a year. It was impossible, that is to say, for a man of his habits, which included a taste for betting, club-life, Turkish baths, and the Criterion bar. When he arrived in London he was still suffering from the effects of the Jezail bullet which at the Battle of Maiwand had shattered his shoulder bone, and the enteric fever which had laid him low in the Base Hospital at Peshawar. The modern tendency in biography to emphasise the regrettable side of human nature may tempt many to read more than is justifiable into that violent phrase which Watson employs in describing London — he speaks of it as "that great cesspool into which all the loungers and idlers of the Empire are irresistibly drained" — but there can be little doubt that during the first two months of 1880, for the last time in his life, Watson sowed a few wild oats.

Economy was equally necessary in the case of the young Sherlock Holmes. We know that Mrs. Hudson's charges were extremely moderate, but it seems scarcely possible that with food, light, and fuel they could hardly, even in the eighties, have been less than £5 a week. We know that Holmes's clientele was at first by no means wealthy, and that his artist's devotion to his profession often induced him to undertake cases which left him out of pocket. However, fame came rapidly, while Watson succeeded in placing his literary work. By 1888, Behrens thinks, all financial troubles were over.

Prosperity at Last

By that time Holmes, as is shown in "The Scandal in Bohemia," had already been of service to several of the crowned heads of Europe; and Behrens is convinced that, in spite of Holmes's quixotism where money was concerned ("My charges are on a fixed scale, I do not vary them except to remit them altogether"), Holmes must have made by 1890 a considerable fortune. The largest sum that we know him to have received is the £6,000 cheque from the Duke of Holderness ("The

Holmes effects a dramatic arrest in "The Adventure of the Dancing Man" (1903).

Priory School Case"); but we know that he was able after his "Return" to buy Watson's practice in Kensington on behalf of his cousin Verner (or Vernet?) for a handsome sum. Nor could he have retired to his bee-keeping in Sussex had he not accumulated a private fortune. The conclusion is inevitable: the most lucrative of his cases were those Watson never chronicled; those in which large financial interests were at stake, such as in '87 the problem of the "Netherland-Sumatra Company and the colossal schemes of Baron Maupertuis." Mr. Blakeney in a footnote ingeniously argues that Holmes might have kept the £1,000 handed to him by the King of Bohemia for expenses, but such a suggestion surely rests upon a grave misapprehension of character.

As every schoolboy ought by this time to know there is a curious difficulty connected with the date of Watson's first marriage. Was it 1886, '87, or '88? This has led to the wildest surmises, even to the reckless suggestion that during one period he was keeping two establishments. Apart from the necessity of clearing the character of one of whom we are sure that whatever record leaps to light he never will be shamed, it is of the first importance to establish the date of Watson's marriage, because, characteristically, he used that date as a sort of B.C. or A.D. in recording the cases of his friend. Yet he often appears as a bachelor in Baker Street when he might have been expected to be living with his wife. It is, therefore, to the pages dealing with "The Sign of Four," which gives us the circumstances of Watson's first marriage, that we instinctively turn first on opening a new book on Sherlockology. I rejoice to say that I am in agreement with Mr. Bell: the marriage took place in October of 1887.

William Gillette
1905

MR. WILLIAM GILETTE.

STEREOSCOPIC CO.
PHOTO BERLIN

The love story of The Great Detective

In the *Strand Magazine* for December 1893, tens of thousands of readers read with sorrow and exasperation of the death of Sherlock Holmes at the foot of the Reichenbach Falls. Conan Doyle, his creator, had grown weary of him and had determined to make an end. Four years later, however, his desire to write a really successful play led his thoughts back to the famous detective and the script was submitted to Beerbohm Tree. Unwilling to make the alterations that the actor-manager wanted, Conan Doyle might well have dropped the project altogether. But the script had found its way to Charles Frohman in New York and Frohman accepted it. Again, re-writing was demanded by William Gillette, who was anxious to play the lead. This time Conan Doyle made no protest and when Gillette cabled: 'May I marry Holmes?' he replied that he could marry him or murder him or do anything else he liked. In the end, he came to feel that Gillette had made a fine play of it and certainly it had a fine reception and along run in America.

In 1901, Gillette brought the play to England. Its premiere was given at Liverpool in the first week of September 1901 and on September 9 it was produced in London at the Lyceum. Gillette had quite frankly plunged Holmes into the melodramatic atmosphere with which patrons of the Lyceum were familiar. One critic, indeed, expressed surprise that Irving himself was not playing the principal role and the management was careful to issue a special notice urging the spectators to be in their seats at eight o'clock precisely, since the interest of the play commenced with the rising of the curtain.

The drama was described as 'a hitherto unpublished episode in the career of the great detective and showing his connection with the Strange Case of Miss Faulkner.' How far it resembles Conan Doyle's original draft we do not know. All that can be said is that the main plot recalls, in a general way, the *Scandal in Bohemia,* and that the interview between Holmes and Moriarty deliberately reproduces some of the earlier passages in *The Final Problem;* but from beginning to end it is melodrama that matters, as the stage directions show. Here is a sample: *Music, Melodramatic, Danger, Keep down pp. Agitato.* No melodrama is complete without a love-interest of some poignancy and the most striking innovation is Holmes' final surrender to Alice Faulkner:

"I suppose — indeed I know — that I love you. I love you. But I know as well what I am — and what you are — I know that no such person as I should ever dream ot being a part of your sweet life! It would be a crime for me to think of such a thing. There is every reason —"

But Alice is not interested in reasons. She gently places her right hand on Holmes' breast and is shortly resting in his arms. And so, with lights fading and music swelling, the curtain falls.

At the end of the first performance Gillette had a tumultuous reception, marred by some interruptions from the gallery in protest against the imperfect audibility of the players.

The critic of *The Times,* presumably A. B. Walkley, wrote a gay and amusing column about the play. Fundamentally, he declared, it was all wrong — no playhouse was large enough to hold the colossal figure of Sherlock Holmes and it was absurd to make him fall in love; the slight disturbance in the gallery he attributed to the myrmidons of Professor Moriarty.

At the time of this first production, I was just preparing to enter a public shool. But the play lived on. Round about 1908 or 1909 I saw it played (and well played) by a touring company at Cambridge. That was long before I had begun to face the problems of Holmesian scholarship; I just enjoyed the evening with the zest proper of an undergraduate.

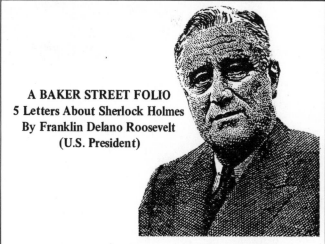

THE EDUCATION OF HOLMES

Sir.— I submit that Sherlock Holmes was almost certainly a member of Magdalene College, Cambridge. His behaviour is hardly consistent with membership of a large college, and his only two friends, Trevor and Musgrave, were throughly representative of the sporting and aristocratic undergraduates of Magdalene in the seventies.

Moreover, while the presence of a bulldog inside Trinity was no doubt always unthinkable, the discipline of Magdalene was not as keen as I hear it is to-day.

There is a difficulty in the fact that in the three adventures of Holmes at Cambridge, Watson appears not to know that he was on familiar ground. But the identity of the guilty student which was discovered in Holmes's busy year, 1895, at "one of our great University towns" was traced by a pellet of the peculiar mixture with which Watts used to fill the long-jump pit at Fenners. I believe this was a secret composition of his own, which he only allowed to be used elsewhere for the University sports at Queens', and which was not available at Oxford.

It is clear from the story of the three students that Holmes recognised the nature of the pellet as soon as he saw it, and it is probable that, besides his boxing and fencing, Holmes did some running and jumping while he was an undergraduate.

Why Holmes did not mention the fact of his familiarity with Cambridge to Watson is not apparent. But undergraduates who have terminated their career after two years are not always anxious to mention the fact, and Holmes, who was certainly an addict of cocaine at a very early age, may very well have met with little encouragement with the college authorities.

Sir H. MACNAGHTEN
Lyminster, Sussex

Dr. Joseph Bell, the real-life original of Sherlock Holmes.

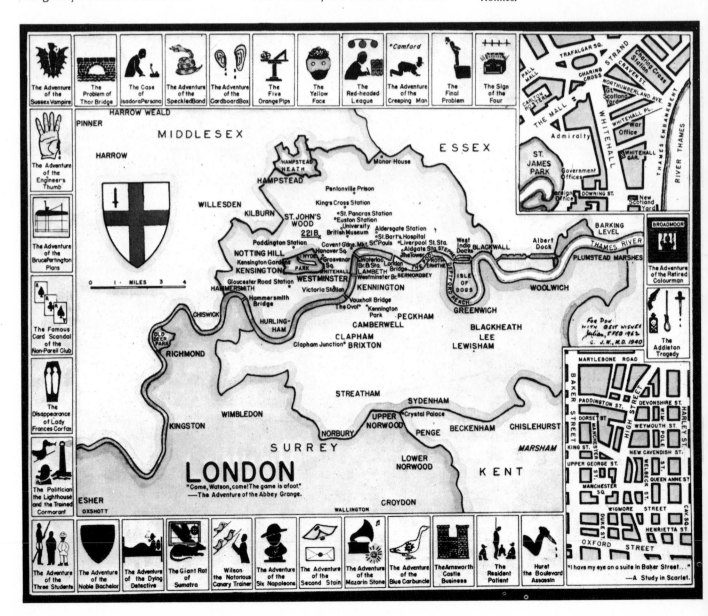

John O'London's Weekly
September 15 1934

SHERLOCK HOLMES AND POE

A correspondent, Mr. W. J. Young, in the British Medical Journal for August 25th, writes to suggest a new origin for Sherlock Holmes. It has often been stated that Conan Doyle got the idea of his creature from a medical man of Edinburgh, Dr. Joseph Bell, and that the methods used by Sherlock Holmes in detection were those of Dr. Bell in diagnosis. Mr. Young reports that he was told in the 'nineties by George Hamilton (then assistant honorary surgeon to Mitchell Banks) that Conan Doyle, at the same time he was a medical student in Edinburgh, "was deeply interested in Poe's detective works, and told Hamilton that he had the idea of writing detective fiction according to the system of Poe, but greatly simplified and brought down to the level of ordinary people." Hamilton was a fellow student with Conan Doyle at Edinburgh.

COLOPHON

Daily Telegraph July 30 1937

SHERLOCK'S HOME
American inquirer's thanks

Sir,— I am delighted to find my interest in Sherlock Holmes adequately shared in England.

In asking your readers for the number of his Baker-street quarters I did not explain I was an American visitor, and several replies have taken me to task rather sharply for having to put the question at all.

But all of my numerous correspondents are most obliging, and many reveal a truly noble zeal in their acquisition of Sherlock Holmes lore. I have letters not only from London, but from almost every English county, from Scotland and from Wales.

For the varied and fascinating information given me I am deeply grateful. You will have noted, though, from the letters you have printed, that there is a slight divergence of opinion. I have as Mr. Holmes's residence 221b, 111, 281b and 112a, Baker-street. The first-named number, however, seems established as that mentioned by Dr. Watson, while 111 is Mr. Vincent Starrett's deduction. My chief regret is that the house no longer exists, wherever it may have stood.

J. S. POPE,
33, Netherhall Gardens, N.W.3.

Two maps by the Sherlockian expert, Dr. Julian Wolff, which graphically illustrate the adventures both at home and abroad.

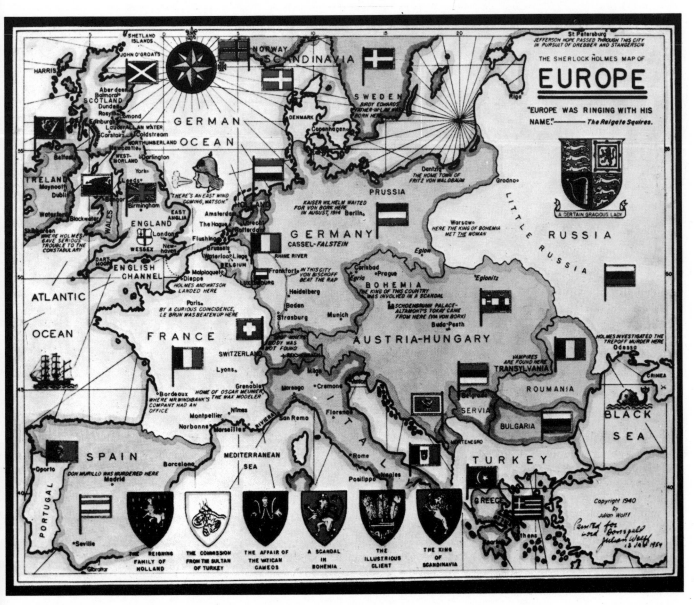

Tears, idle tears

When I had read in my evening paper *"The Ministry of Food have appointed their own Big Three from Scotland Yard to deal with the Black Market,"* how hard it was to prevent my thoughts from wandering to that April evening long ago in Baker Street when the blurred lamp-light was reflected from the puddles, and only a single four-wheeled cab could be seen in the far distance driving furiously up the deserted thoroughfare! How hard, did I say? It was so hard that I made no effort. I permitted my thoughts to wander as they would.

There they sat, the long lithe figure of the detective leaning back in his arm-chair, complaining with some bitterness to his friend and biographer that only the most sensational cases were admitted to the chronicles, while many a more brilliant triumph of deduction (like the Mysterious Affair of the Tattooed Wharfinger) had never been revealed to the most importunate patron of the *Strand Magazine.*

And the flustered client . . .

Very beautiful she was when, pushing up her thick black veil she revealed her features stained with weeping, haggard with an anxiety which gave place of indignation and bewilderment when Holmes observed quietly: "And what has brought you to see me, Lady Blottingham?"

She bridled.

"How can you possibly know who I am, Mr. Holmes?"

"Madam, if you wished to conceal your identity you should have removed your family crest from your pocket handkerchief."

She blushed.

"A terrible thing has happened, Mr. Holmes! The Blottingham onions have been stolen."

"The famous rope?"

"None other."

"Renowned among all the *cognescenti* of Belgravia?"

"It is indeed."

"Coveted by all the gourmets of Bloomsbury?"

She nodded.

"They were bequeathed to me by my father, the Duke of Matlock, just before he died of a chill last autumn. He grew them on his own allotment in Hanover Square. As you know, they are almost irreplaceable at the present moment, for the new crop has only recently been planted. I was to wear them at the Free Bulgarian Ball at the Grosvenor Hotel. They would then have been raffled and we hoped to raise a thousand pounds for the cause."

"Kindly narrate the circumstances."

She narrated them. Every night the vegetables had been locked up in a small safe, the key of which she kept under her pillow. No one but her ninety-year-old maid knew the secret. The key had not been taken, but the safe was rifled, there were marks on the window-sill, footprints on the drive and on the carrot-bed, and lettuce-shoots were trampled down.

"And the gate and the railings?"

"They have been turned into Hurricanes."

"You have informed Scotland Yard?"

"I did so immediately, but so far they have been unable to assist me."

She left, still weeping.

Holmes (I think) rose quietly and went to the bookcase, took down a fat red volume and studied it intently.

"We are in deep waters, Watson, very deep. But hullo, whom have we here?"

Lestrade? Of course it was Lestrade. Confident, but not over confident. Gifted, but alas! uninspired.

"I think we shall soon lay our man by the heels, Mr. Holmes."

What have you done so far?"

"We have interviewed the managers of every large hotel in London and the provinces, and drawn a cordon round Soho. Every well-known fruiterer is being watched night and day. Shoulders of mutton are being shadowed by officials of the Ministry of Food."

"You suspect the Black Market?"

The great man put the tips of his fingers together and slowly shook his head.

"Come, come, Mr. Holmes, you are trifling with me."

"I was never more serious in my life."

He goes away downhearted. The two friends are left together. Holmes borrows a match. The room grows poisonous with the fumes of shag.

"Have you any ideas, Watson?"

"None whatever."

"Yet to me the case seems remarkably simple. Are you prepared for a little expedition?"

He is.

"Do I need my revolver, Holmes?"

"An assegai will be ample."

They set out.

Need I continue? The briefest summary will surely suffice. The visit to the great mansion, occupied except for one small wing by the Ministry of Integral Complications and Co-ordinated Affairs; the interview with Lord Blottingham, aristocratic to his finger-tips and a former Secretary of State for War; the sudden fainting-fit which overcame the great detective; the pulling away of a curtain as he staggers wildly, to

reveal an unsuspected door; the fury of Lord
Blottingham, who snatches a knobkerrie from the wall;
the brief fight; the triumph of Watson; the little room
redolent of savoury suppers with its improvised
kitchen apparatus; the discovery of all that is left of
the famous Blottingham rope; the copy of Mrs.
Beeton's book open at the words "Take two large
onions"; the confession of the humiliated nobleman;
the byves, the prison van; all these things will be
guessed immediately by every student of the old
magician's ways.

And Watson's naive perplexity . . . .

"The footprints, Holmes, and the scratches on the
window-sill?"

"A mere blind, Watson. And a very obvious one.
Not in the least difficult for a man of athletic build
who has been a big-game hunter as well as a politician.
Besides I suspected him immediately. Amongst the list
of clubs to which Lord Blottingham belongs I note The
Gastronomic Circle in Pall Mall and The Epicures in
St. James's Square. They were both, I think, bombed a
year ago. And now, if you care to accompany me, I
believe there is an excellent concert at the Boeotian
Hall."

But they are both crying a little as they go away.

THE OLD TIN BOX
by Jay Finlay Christ

In the vaults of Cox was an old
    tin box
    With Watson's name on its lid.
What wouldn't we pay for that box
    today
    And the secret notes there hid?

Old Russian dame, Ricoletti the
    lame,
    The famous aluminium crutch;
For Alicia, the cutter, the parsley
    in butter,
    What would you give for such?

Story of Randall, Darlington scandal,
    The coptic patriarchs,
The opal tiara, the Addleton barrow—
    Dollars? or francs? or marks?

The tale of the pinch of Victor
    Lynch,
    The furniture warehouse mob,
The case at the Hague, the murder
    at Prague
    The powderless Margate job.

The giant rat, the cardinal's hat,
    The Patersons (first name Grice),
The cormorant's bill, the Hammer-
    ford will—
    We'd take 'em at *any* price.

The Phillimore fella who sought an
    umbrella,
    The steamer Friesland (Dutch);
For Col. Carruthers or Atkinson
    brothers
    One *never* could give too much.

The Vatican case and its cameo face,
    The slithering, unknown worm,
The Abergavenny were none too
    many —
    Where *is* this Cox's firm?

Oh, wonderful box in the vaults of
    Cox!
    You come with a touch of salt!
But I offer two blocks of choicest
    stocks
    For the treasure of Cox's vault.

New York, 1946

Eille Norwood-there goes the master

The Master in drag! Eille Norwood as Holmes disguised as an old lady in "The Greek Interpreter."

Over eighty years old, he sits in a beautiful sunlit room, looking out over a green lawn, pleasantly fringed with fine trees and bright flowers.

His real name is Brett, but to tens of thousands who saw him on the stage and screen before, during, and after the first world war, he is best known as Eille Norwood — or Sherlock Holmes.

Twenty-six years after he starred in the first of nearly fifty Holmes films, he looks remarkably like the great detective in retirement. A finely cut profile and magnetic eyes add to the deception. And in a cupboard in his room hangs the same dressing-gown which he wore as Holmes on both stage and screen.

Although there have been many other Sherlocks — Saintsbury, Gillette, Arthur Wontner, Clive Brook, Basil Rathbone — no one else has ever played the part in both plays and films. He modelled his performance on Sidney Paget's famous illustrations and Sir Arthur Conan Doyle was so delighted that he revealed to the actor a secret which he entrusted to no one else, it was the simple story of how Holmes got his name. He was named, it appears, after two cricketers — Sherlock and Holmes.

When, in 1921, the Stoll company decided to produce a film series of the famous adventures, Norwood was at once invited to play the leading role. Into the early hours of the morning he studied each story, memorising the habits and behaviour of Holmes. By day he learned how to handle a violin, and sat for

hours in front of a mirror, testing make-up. Then he shaved the hair from his temples and reported to the studios at Cricklewood.

At first Director Maurice Elvey disagreed with Eille Norwood's interpretation of the role. But Norwood was insistent. "Let's film your way first, then mine," he suggested. So they took several shots of each scene, and next day went to the studio theatre to see their first day's work on the screen. Elvey readily agreed that Norwood was right. "I'll never tell you to do anything again," he said. "You're perfect."

Studying the first script at home, Norwood had been horrified to read the words: "Enter Sherlock Holmes, in a white beard." He protested strongly. "But Holmes would never have done that," he said.

It was obvious that the film executives had little idea what Holmes *would* have done, and when Norwood outlined his plans for disguises, they were dubious. Jeffrey Bernard, production chief of Stolls, told him he would never be able to disguise his height and appearance.

Visitors were not allowed in the studios, so next day when Jeffrey Bernard noticed a little taxi driver standing on the studio set, he at once sent someone to remove him. The taxi driver insisted, in the best Cockney, that his taxi was outside, and that he was only watching. For several minutes technicians argued with him, then he drew himself up to his full height, and revealed himself as Eille Norwood.

After that they grew used to his masterly make-up, but never knew what disguise he would adopt next. In the scripts it still said "In a white beard," but Norwood adopted the identical disguises worn by Holmes in the stories. When he appeared as a bald headed little Japanese opium addict, the studio doorman refused to allow him inside. He wouldn't believe it was Eille Norwood.

Other disguises followed thick and fast, in true Holmes tradition, and the actor began to delight in surprising people — even his family — in unusual make-up. For *A Scandal in Bohemia* he donned a round bald head, bushy white eyebrows and glasses. In *The Greek Interpreter* he became an old woman. For *Black Peter* he was a skipper. In *The Sign of Four* he appeared as a one-eyed organ grinder. Nose wax, twisted lips, padded cheeks, and the artful use of grease paint and eye-shadow assisted him. He made-up quickly, altered his height, his breathing, his gestures, his walk, and his whole personality. Audiences might guess, but they could never be sure which was Holmes and which wasn't, until the great moment in each adventure when some unlikely character whipped off his disguise and revealed the familiar beaked nose and clear-cut profile of the great detective.

The late Sir Arthur Conan Doyle has revealed that Holmes often proved an embarrassment to him. People began to think that he had written no other books. So it was with Eille Norwood. For although he had been a West End theatre star for some years, the pictures brought him a fresh and greater public who knew him only as Holmes — with the dressing-gown, the pipe, the violin and the untidy Baker Street rooms.

Outside the giant Capitol Cinema on Broadway they pasted up an immense coloured poster of him,

The Master in disguise again. In "His Last Bow" Norwood appeared as Holmes playing an Irish-American spy.

heralding the success of the films in America. These were the days before James Mason's pictures invaded New York, when Eille Norwood's films were shown not only in America, but in nearly every foreign country.

In Britain, cinema owners rushed to book the Holmes series. And soon Eille Norwood himself became Sherlock Holmes to millions of people. They wrote him hundreds of letters, some of them asking him to solve their problems, others congratulating him on his performance. They told him how to outwit Moriarty, what sort of disguises he should adopt, they asked him to tea, and they sent him letters written in invisible ink.

From all over the world the letters poured in, addressed not only to Holmes and Eille Norwood, but to I. N. Norwood, I. Lee Norwood, Pillo Norwood, and even on one occasion to Ellinor Wood. And when he walked down the street, or took a stroll in the direction of the Savage Club or the Garrick, people pointed him out and said: "Look — there goes Sherlock Holmes!"

One day he entered a crowded railway carriage and had hardly sat down before the whisper went round. He fled, and dived quickly into the next compartment, only to discover that it was full of small boys. From them there was no escape, for now he had to be Holmes himself, and no mere actor. But Norwood says he enjoyed the journey, and as there were no grown-ups present, he gave a good performance, to the delight of his youthful audience.

Like Holmes, Eille Norwood has always been keenly observant and interested in unusual things. A bird lover, he can imitate the call or song of almost every bird. And his ingenuity as a West End stage producer is apparent today, when many of the effects used are still the original ones which he devised. And also like Holmes, he has always loved the unusual problem — the mysteries of life which take some solving.

To him goes the credit for having introduced the more difficult, or "twisted" type of crossword puzzle clue. For twelve years he never failed to compose three puzzles a week for the *Daily Express*, and only illness prevents him from doing them now, for Holmes himself had no more agile a brain. Holmes, one feels sure, would have delighted in dashing off tricky crosswords in the Norwood manner, and calling them 'elementary.'

Today Eille Norwood sits puffing his pipe, recalling a life of remarkable achievement. He has not seen the more modern Holmes films, for he no longer goes out. But somehow one feels that he might not approve of them, for the mysteries and adventures which the great detective solved lie in a byegone age of hansom cabs, flickering gaslight, wing collars, and dog carts, and the new Holmes might seem strangely out of place in an atom-conscious world.

Punch October 17 1923

AT THE PLAY
"The Return of Sherlock Holmes"
(Princes Theatre)

Mr. J.E. Harold Terry and Mr. Arthur Rose have made a play out of material drawn from Sir Arthur Conan Doyle's later Sherlock Holmes' stories, and have done their patchwork in a neat and lively manner, providing a quite sound entertainment even for the sophisticated.

Perhaps they have rather piled it on. Poor Holmes looking an older and sadder man, and I regret to say having recourse to the morphine needle to keep his immense brain in first-rate working order, and still handicapped by the egregious Watson, has no fewer than fourteen criminals to deal with out of the cast of twenty two.

Mr. Ellie Norwood's performance as Holmes seemed to me admirable, and the whole production, for which he was responsible, ingenious and competent. This kind depends more, I think, upon production than upon any very great subtlety of acting.

Mr. H.G. Stoker's Watson seemed well-done, with the right degree of affectionate, admiring stupidity. Mr. Lauderdale Maitland's Colonel Moran was immense, while Mr. Stafford Hilliard (Profennis), Mr. Eric Stanley (Milverton) and Miss Molly Kerr (Lady Frances) all seemed to me adequate.

Colonel Moran's gang alone seemed rather tiresome and unconvincing.

Of its kind, "The Return of Sherlock Holmes" is certainly a good thing.

Eille Norwood as The Master in "The Return of Sherlock Holmes" at the Prince's Theatre in 1923. He is having a wax model made of himself to fool Colonel Moran.

The passing of Sherlock Holmes

His obituary as it might have appeared in "The Times"

The death is announced at North Friston, near Eastbourne, of Mr. Sherlock Holmes, the eminent Criminologist and Investigator, President of the South Sussex Apiarist Society, and Corresponding Secretary to the National Beekeepers' Union. He was in his ninety-third year; and there is little doubt that but for his characteristic disregard of the occupational risks of this last hobby he would have lived to become a centenarian.

"The creatures know my methods," he would often observe to visitors as he walked without veil or gloves between the orderly rows of his hives. Yet he overestimated their obedience, and it was an irritant poison caused by one of these dangerous insects, possibly an Italian Queen, that undermined his iron constitution in the end, and was the immediate occasion of his demise.

His white hair and only slightly stooping figure had long been objects of veneration both to the passing motorist and to all residents of the countryside between Birling Gap and Newhaven.

He was particularly interested in the formation and history of dew ponds, and might often have been seen returning to his little farmhouse with a bundle of fossils taken from the chalk or a nosegay of downland flowers.

His later years were but little disturbed by occurrences either terrible or bizarre, but we must except from this statement the sudden appearance (narrated by himself) of *Cyanea Capillata*, the giant jellyfish, which, at the foot of the Seven Sisters, stung to death Mr. Fitzroy Macpherson, and came very near to baffling the old Investigator's deductive powers. Otherwise, his closing years were passed in quietitude. Every evening he was accustomed to listen to the Third or the Home Programme of the B.B.C., especially the musical portions. For Light Programmes, and especially for the feature entitled "Dick Barton," he was wont to express a profound contempt.

Birth, parentage, and education

Sherlock Spencer Tracy Holmes was born in 1854, the second son of Sir Stateleight Holmes of Carshalton in Surrey. The family was descended from a long line of country squires, and Sir Stateleigh's mother was the sister of Vernet the French artist. Sherlock himself was educated at St. Peter's School and Pembridge College, Camford, where the rooms he occupied (now held by the Director of Theological Studies in that College) are often pointed out with pride and gratification by the present Master.

He took little part in the academic or sporting life of his contemporaries and made few friends; but those whom he did know never forgot him and lived to be thankful for the fact. Two of the most eminent were the late Colonel Reginald Musgrave, M.F.H., of Hurlston, and Admiral Victor Trevor, K.C.B., both of whom he had assisted at critical junctures in their youth, and it is safe to say that but for these early acquaintanceships neither the whereabouts of the lost crown of Charles I nor the log-book of the *Gloria Scott* would ever have been made known to the public. It was, indeed, Admiral Trevor's father who actually suggested to Holmes in his early days the vocation which he afterwards so brilliantly followed, using the following remarkable prophetic words: "I don't know how you managed this, Mr. Holmes, but it seems to me that all the detectives of fact and of fancy would be children in your hands. That's your line of life, sir; and you may take the word of a man who has seen something of the world."

He spoke no more than the truth. Dying a few months later, with little more time than to say that the papers were in the back drawer of the Japanese cabinet, Mr. Trevor could not foresee that his son's friend was destined to become almost a legendary figure, the hero and idol of two generations of mankind, and the scourge of evil-doers throughout what was once called the civilised globe.

Wanderings abroad

No detective can have travelled more widely than the late Mr. Holmes, nor on errands so mysterious, not to say sinister, and verging on the grotesque. Summoned to Odessa to unravel the Trepoff murder, he was equally successful in solving the tragedy of the Atkinson brothers at Trincomalee. Rome knew him at the enquiry into the sudden death of Count Tosca; Lyons, when he had penetrated the collosal scandals of Baron Maupertins in connection with the Netherland Sumatra Company. In the interval between his supposed death in Switzerland and his reappearance in London he made journeys through Persia, looked in at Mecca, rendered assistance to the Khalifa of Khartoum, visited Lhasa, and spent some time with the Grand Lama of Tibet. It is a pity that the details of these expeditions are for most part wrapped in a veil of impenetrable secrecy, which, unless the great tin box bequeathed to the British Museum is opened by Mr. Attlee or some future Prime Minister, may never be lifted.

Work at home

But in spite of these foreign pilgrimages, Holmes was

able to undertake in this country a series of investigations which made him for more than twenty years, and later at intervals, the terror of the metropolitan underworld, the knighterrant of suburban London, and the constant corrector of the stupidities of Scotland Yard.

This department, especially during the middle 'nineties, appears to have had only two consistent policies, of which the first was complacent error and the second unutterable bewilderment. Holmes revolutionised its procedure, and we may note as

Blackmail and forgery were rife. The robbery of the most famous piece of jewellery in the world was an almost hourly occurrence. Agents of mysterious secret societies, thirsting for revenge, haunted the docks and the purlieus of Soho. Wills and the plans of submarines were constantly disappearing, and no treaty with a foreign power was safe for more than a moment in its desk.

The new order
To all these manifestations of the villainous and the

Illustrated by Wyndham Robinson

evidence of this that the old daguerreotypes of Athelney Jones, Gregson, and Lestrade, which once adorned its portrait galley, have long ago had their faces turned to the wall. It is a pity that the projected work by Assistant Commissioner Stanley Hopkins, O.B.E., entitled "My Master's Voice" remained uncompleted at the time of the Nether Wallop Mystery, when that able officer met his end after a dastardly assault from the blow-pipe of a Nicaraguan dwarf.

If ever a man was called for to meet the hour, Sherlock Holmes, in the heyday of his triumphs, was that man. For England, during the last decade of the 19th century, was in danger of submersion beneath an almost unprecedented wave of crime. Criminals of Herculean strength and stature, gifted with a well-nigh superhuman cunning, had spread a network of villainy throughout the land.

macabre, Holmes opposed a technique, entirely novel and entirely his own. It may be sub-divided and tabulated as follows:

1. Chemical Analysis; 2. Analytical Deduction; 3. Tobacco; 4. Bouts of Contemplation; 5. Feverish Energy; 6. The Minute Examination of Scratches; 7. Omniscience; 8. Cocaine.

And to these should possibly be added the cross-indexing of important cases, the music of the violin, the employment of a hoard of street Arabs as agents, and the constant use of the Agony Columns of the Daily Press. The result was a purer air in the streets of London, a sense of relief in the suburbs from Kensington to Whitechapel, from Hampstead to Norwood, and the rescue of many an ill-used girl from death or worse than death in the Home Counties and the more distant provinces.

Repeatedly also the Government of the day was

saved from ruin. We need only mention in this connection the temporary loss of the Bruce Partington Submarine plans in 1895, and the fear that they might have been sold to a Foreign Power. "You may take it from me," said Mr. Holmes's brother in speaking of them, "that naval warfare becomes impossible when in the radius of a Bruce Partington's operation." Happily for the future of this country, Mr. Holmes succeeded in recovering the plans.

By the close of the century, the agency which he established had become world-famous. Many were the nights when the feet of a flustered client would patter along the flagstones of Baker Street, or the spirited horse of some hastily driven four-wheeler would be reined to its haunches at his door.

The sound of his violin would float out into the foggy atmosphere, punctuated by the pistol shots with which he pock-marked the pattern V.R. from his sofa on the opposite wall of his sitting-room.

A bundle of letters from the sister of his landlady (recently discovered on a bomb site) is ample evidence of the admiration not unmingled with awe which he inspired in the whole of her family.

The influence of Lord Watson

But it is impossible to deal adequately with the great detective's achievements unless we acknowledge the peculiar debt that he owed during the greater part of his active career to his old friend and colleague, the late Lord Watson of Staines. Lord Watson, it will be remembered, died suddenly last year, after a particularly violent attack in the House of Lords upon certain provisions of the National Health Bill. Eminent alike as a physician and an orator, he is none the less even more likely to incur the gratitude of posterity as the constant companion and intermittent (though mystified) biographer of Mr. Sherlock Holmes.

"How do you know that?"

"I followed you."

"I saw no one."

"That is what you may expect to see when I follow you."

Yet indeed it was Lord Watson himself, wondering, shadowy, yet observant, who followed Holmes. Without him, Holmes would have remained a mysterious, almost a visionary character: known to the police forces of the world, familiar to the Courts and the aristocracies of Europe, the condescending patron of Prime Ministers, and of the humbler clients whom he chose to assist, yet occult from the observation of the public at large. For publicity was a thing he disdained, and only in the case of Lord Watson, especially in the privacy of the rooms which they shared, did he throw off the mantle of obscurity that screened his personal habits from the eyes of men.

Never, we think, has so great a privilege been so enthusiastically enjoyed. Lord Watson was *par excellence* a hero-worshipper. He had nothing to learn of Plato or Boswell in this respect. To be baffled was his glory, to be astounded his perennial delight. Sitting with his medical dictionary just out of the line of pistol fire, he revelled in the deductive processes by which the great detective inferred the whole of a visiting client's character from a button, a whisker, a

watch, or a boot. There are many who say that Lord Watson was an inaccurate historian. There are cavillers (and Holmes himself was one of them) who have suggested that he embellished fact with fiction, and dipped his brush in melodrama instead of depicting the portrait of a living man. It is impossible to pursue all these charges in detail. Yet one or two comments are not out of place.

Holmes on the trail

Curiously enough, his biographer's presentation does not always redound to the advantage of Holmes. Lord Watson was bemused by metaphors. His mind was influenced beyond all reason by images of the chase. Time after time, for instance, he seems to have been obsessed with the idea that Mr. Holmes was a kind of dog.

"As I watched him I was irresistibly reminded of a pure-blooded well-trained foxhound as it dashes backwards and forwards through the covert, whining in its eagerness until it comes across the lost scent . . ."

"His nostrils seemed to dilate with a purely animal lust for the chase, and his mind was so absolutely

concentrated upon the matter before him that a question or remark fell unheeded upon his ears, or at the most only provoked a quick impatient snarl in reply . . ."

"He was out on the lawn, in through the window, round the room, and up into the bedroom, for all the world like a dashing foxhound drawing a cover . . ."

"Like an old hound who hears the View Holloa . . ."

Hard indeed it is to reconcile these phrases with the picture of the tall, dignified, sombrely-attired figure whom we know so well from his portraits in the Strand Magazine, dressed in frock coat or ulster; the finely chiselled features, the pale intellectual forehead surmounted by the silk or Derby hat. Even the deerstalker of his more rustic peregrinations does not warrant the perpetual comparison of Mr. Holmes to a denizen of the hunting kennel: and we can only feel the idolatry has here overstepped its bounds, and trespassed on the realm of caricature.

On the other hand, Holmes (as stated in a previous paragraph) was omniscient. Lord Watson must have known this. Yet he denies it. He makes Holmes attribute this particular gift (or "specialism" as he called it) to Sir Mycroft, the detective's elder brother, but Sherlock (as a hundred instances will testify) had it, too. Let a single example suffice.

Knowledge of literature

From what motive one cannot guess, whether from envy or for the sake of whimsical exaggeration, Lord Watson in one memoir states that Sherlock's knowledge of Literature was *nil*. In another he makes Holmes quote Goethe twice, discuss miracle plays, comment on Richter, Hafiz, and Horace, and remark of Athelney Nones: "He has occasional glimmerings of reason. *'Il n'y a pas des sots si incommodes que ceux qui ont de Pesprit!'*"

It has even been conjectured, though wrongly, from this evidence of wide culture that Mr. Holmes was attracted by the decadent aesthetic movement of the 'nineties. But a careful search through the pages of the Yellow Book fails to reveal any poem or prose contribution from his pen, and the whole tenor of his life seems to remove him entirely from the world in which Dowson, Symons, and Aubrey Beardsley and the other ghosts of the old Cafe Royal lived and moved. He is never mentioned by Sir William Rothenstein or Six Max Beerbohm in any of their reminiscences of the period. As a literary figure he remains enigmatic and aloof. Yet from Lord Watson's narrative, however melodramatic, however inaccurate, there does emerge the definite picture of a man; and (if we are prepared to make allowances for the occasional eccentricities of the writer) a man who must be very like the real Holmes.

A Great Englishman

To continue the actual narrative of his known career, Sherlock Holmes was offered a knighthood in 1902 but refused it. He took up Government work in the period immediately preceding the first World War, and was instrumental in foiling the notorious Von Bork, one of the most devoted agents of the Kaiser. For this he was again offered a knighthood which he again refused.

He had a profound knowledge of chemistry, and a grip of iron, was an expert boxer and swordsman, and a voluminous writer. His most popular and widely-read works are those on *The Polyphonic Motets of Lassus*, his two short *Monographs on Ears*, originally published in the Antropological Journal, his brochures on *The Tracing of Footsteps, with some Remarks upon the Uses of Plaster as a Preserver of Impresses*, his *Influence of a Trade on the Form of a Hand*, his *Essay on the Distinction of the Ashes of Various Tobaccos*, and his *Handbook of Bee Culture, with some Observations upon the Segregation of the Queen*.

It is one of fate's ironies that a failure to observe some of his own precepts, laid down in the last book, may have brought about the close of a life ever devoted to his country's good. His form and lineaments, together with those of Lord Watson, have long been familiar in waxen effigy at Madam Tussaud's Exhibition, not far from his old lodgings. A sturdy moralist, if not a devout Churchman, he was also an ardent Democrat, a believer in the close union of the English-speaking races, a hater of the colour bar, and a despiser of the trappings of pomp and power. He may well have been said, in the words of Kipling, to have walked with Kings nor lost the common touch. He was unmarried.

A dramatic moment from "The Adventure of the Three Garridebs" by one of the later "Strand Magazine" illustrators, Howard K. Elcock (January 1925).

The Sunday Graphic October 10 1943

SHERLOCK HOLMES - HIS CREATOR'S SECRET BY JOHN BROPHY

Of all his writing, Conan Doyle thought most highly of the historical romances like "The White Company". He also put an immense amount of effort and goodwill into redressing miscarriages of justice, such as the conviction of Oscar Slater, and the last years of his life were devoted to spiritualism.

But there is no doubt that his name survives, and will survive, as the creator of Sherlock Holmes.

Now, it is well-known that Conan Doyle developed the Sherlock Holmes method from the inductive reasoning used by a surgeon, Dr. Joseph Bell, in his lectures at Edinburgh Infirmary. But Mr. Hesketh Pearson in his lively and sensible biography ("Conan Doyle" Methuen), tells us that there was another and much more unusual real-life original of Sherlock Holmes.

This was George Budd, a medical student with Doyle who afterwards worked with him in practice. Budd was a man of ideas, an inventor, half-inspired, half-crazy. He played rugby, and apparently the only reason he was not capped was "the savage fury of his game."

Budd lacked the philosophic calm of Sherlock Holmes, whose first name, by the way, was originally drafted as "Shillingford" and "Sherington" and whose surname came from admiration for Oliver Wendell Holmes.

Conan Doyle himself seems to have been imaginative only within strict limits. Wholly Irish in ancestry, born and educated in Scotland, he was a typical nineteenth century 'Englishman', tall, strong, athletic and rather simple in character.

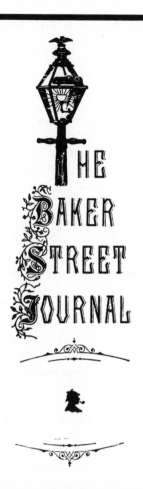

The Friends of the Baker Street Irregulars and Affiliated Scion Societies

This is to certify that *..S. Meredith Western...*, a subscriber to THE BAKER STREET JOURNAL in good and accepted standing, is one of *The Friends of the Baker Street Irregulars and Affiliated Scion Societies* throughout the land, and, as such, is entitled to "go everywhere, see everything, overhear everyone" in the doings of these organizations devoted to the perpetuation and magnification of the name and fame of Sherlock Holmes, subject only to the tests and qualifications imposed, respectively, as to due erudition and scholarship in the Law and the Canon.

Attested, for The Baker Street Journal, this 31 day of July, 19 48.

Ben Abramson
Publisher

Edgar W. Smith
Editor

QUESTIONNAIRE FOR ENTRY IN THE ILLUSTRIOUS CLIENTS SHERLOCK HOLMES SOCIETY of Indianapolis, Ind; USA

1 What do you consider is the middle name of Dr. John H. Watson? Why?

2 Write an original paper on Holmes. It may be any type but parody.

3 In what part, anatomically and locally, was Dr. Watson wounded? When? With What?

4 Who is or was?:
   a. Irene Adler?
   b. Godfrey Norton?
   c. Culverton Smith?
   d. Professor Moriarty (in detail)?
   e. Colonel Moran (in detail)?
   f. Mrs. Cecil Forrester?
   g. Sherlock Holmes?

5 Who was Sherlock Holmes's brother? Junior or elder? By how many years?

6 What was the name of the 1st Holmes Tale, where was it published, in what and when?

7 Name as many of the Holmes-Watson emulators from memory as possible?

8 Where were the unrecorded Tales kept? In what?

9 Name some of the unrecorded Tales? From memory.

10 Are you prepared to spend a certain amount of time and money in the name of Sherlock Holmes?
April 5 1948

The Times February 6 1949

CONAN DOYLE: CRUSADER BY DOROTHY L. SAYERS

It cannot be helped. For all the world, and probably for all time, the fame of Conan Doyle must stand coupled with the name of Sherlock Holmes. That Doyle resented this, that he came to loathe Holmes, that he pushed him over the Reichenbach Falls in the vain hope of getting rid of him, is sad but true, and is only superficially inconsistent with Mr. Dickson Carr's assertion that, in a very real sense, "Sherlock Holmes was Conan Doyle."

Even without Doyle's own convincing detective work in the Edalji and Slater cases, we should know that any character so vital as this must have been vitalised from within, not founded on external observation only. But the creator is the whole of his creation and more; he cannot be identified with any one part of it. And if, while he is intent on exploring and expressing some new part of his creative personality, he is badgered into returning to that earlier thing which he has for the time being happily written out of his system, spontaneity is hampered, zest destroyed, and delight turned into weariness. One cannot but regret that Doyle's enjoyment of his greatest creation was thus poisoned for him, because he was a man who liked to throw himself with generous enthusiasm into whatever he undertook. His story, from its struggling and impecunious beginnings to its wealthy and honoured close, is the adventure of an eager, chivalrous and courageous nature, accepting life in all its manifestations with an enormous gusto. It was this gusto which roared out superabundantly in "Professor Challenger," and which caused such historical novels as "Micah Clarke" and "The White Company" to be taken, (greatly to his annoyance) as ebullient cloak-and-sword romances, rather than as the sober period-evocations which he intended them to be.

However conscientiously he steeped himself in his source-material, he could never be dry-as-dust; what 'got across' was not the accidents of study but his own substantial vitality. That is why his most triumphant success in this sort is the "Brigadier Gerard" series, with the bravura which he found in his French original.

Daily Express December 14, 1949

A MAGAZINE DIES — AND A FIFTY YEAR SECRET COMES OUT

Sir Arthur Conan Doyle wrote on the back of this picture of Sherlock Holmes: "This comes nearest to my conception of what Holmes really looks like."

The sketch, by artist Frank Wiles, was found last night in the files of the Strand Magazine, which is to close down next February.

When Sherlock Holmes first appeared in the new sixpenny Strand Magazine in 1891, Conan Doyle was paid £35 a story.

By the time the last of the Holmes adventures appeared in 1927, the Strand was paying more than £800 for the British rights only.

With illustrations on nearly every page, and highly paid short stories (Kipling was paid £100 for one thousand words), the Strand was the first of the modern magazines.

It was so popular in its early years that there were queues at the railway bookstalls for each new number. With no motor cars, no cinemas, no radio, when the telephone was still a novelty and income tax was 6d in the £, the sixpenny Strand magazine was selling 350,000 copies.

Macdonald Hastings, its editor, said last night: "But the Strand could not keep up with the quicker tempo of a new age."

Time January 2, 1950

DEATH OF A TRADITION

Before the publishing house of George Newnes Ltd., just off London's Strand, a hansom cab stopped and out stepped an elegant young man in top-hat and frock coat. He was Arthur Conan Doyle, come to deliver the manuscript of a short story entitled *A Scandal in Bohemia.* Published in the six-month-old *Strand* magazine, in July 1891, the story's hero was a sleuth named Sherlock Holmes. He was an instant hit and so was the *Strand.*

For 36 years, Conan Doyle wrote exclusively for the *Strand*, in a literary company that has seldom been equalled by any periodical. Shrewd, mustached Herbert Greenough Smith, the *Strand's* editor for four decades, gave his readers the best in Britain to provide "wholesome and harmless entertainment to hard-working people."

It was the *Strand* that first published Rudyard Kipling's *Puck of Pook's Hill*, H. G. Wells's *The First Men in the Moon* and W. W. Jacobs' "Night Watchman" stories; it gave a head start to such other up-&-coming writers and illustrators as P. G. Wodehouse, Agatha Christie, A. E. W. Mason, George Bernard Shaw, Max Beerbohm, Osbert Lancaster and Sidney Paget.

The Sunday Times February 26
1950

BUJITSU IN BAKER STREET
BY RICHARD HUGHES

Sherlock Holmes enthusiasts
around the world will doubtless
be excited to know that the first
Oriental branch of the Baker Street
Irregulars, The Baritsu Chapter, has
been formed in Tokyo under the
Occupation.

As the Nipponese chapter included leading Japanese, it can be
said that a common devotion to the
memory of The Master of Baker
Street was the means, peace treaty
or no, of first restoring Japan cul-
turally to the comity of nations.

The late Count Makino, one of
Japan's distinguished Elder States-
men, who was her representative at
Versailles and narrowly escaped
assassination by the militarists in
the 1936 Tokyo army mutiny, was
one of the foundation members of
the Baritsu chapter. He had a profound knowledge of the Holmes-
Watson saga, and his scholarly

Carleton Hobbs, Radio's Sherlock Holmes, and Chief Inspector Robert
Fabian of Scotland Yard, unveiling a plaque presented by the Baritsu
Chapter of the Baker Street Irregulars of Tokyo. The event, at the
Criterion Long Bar in London, took place in January 1953 and was
arranged by Richard Hughes.

grandson, Kenichi Yoshida, son of the present Prime Minister, a Cambridge graduate and another member of the Baritsu chapter, testifies to his late grandfather's angry rejection of modern Western detective mysteries and intense re-reading of the original Holmes stories.

On his death-bed last year, the ailing Count Makino wrote a learned paper for the opening meeting of the Baritsu chapter. He clarified the doubts of Holmesian students over the use of the curious word "baritsu," from which the Tokyo chapter takes its name, by Holmes in the "Adventure of the Empty House." Students will remember that Holmes, explaining his miraculous return from the dead to the shaken Watson, credited his escape from the long, murderous arms of Professor Moriarty to his "knowledge of baritsu, or the Japanese system of wrestling," which enabled him to hurl the arch-criminal into the Reichenbach Falls.

The word has been loosely accepted by students as an alternative Japanese term for "jujitsu." But, as Count Makino pointed out, there is no such word as "baritsu" in the Japanese language. He suggested in his brilliant paper, that its appearance in the Holmes saga was just another of Dr. Watson's numerous errors as chronicler.

"What Holmes actually said," wrote Count Makino, "was: 'I have some knowledge of bujitsu, which includes the Japanese system of wrestling.' Bujitsu is the Japanese word for the martial arts, which in addition to jujitsu embrace the study of archery, fencing, spearmanship, pike-thrusting, long and short swordsmanship, military fortification and the firing of cannon, muskets and small arms.

Holmes as Specialist

"Sherlock Holme's proficiency in all these highly specialised arts is well known. We know his weakness for pock-marking the walls of his apartment with patriotic initials; his knowledge of airguns was at least equal to that of Colonel Sebastian Moran; we have a glimpse of his acquaintance with pike and spear in the 'Adventure of Black Peter,' in which he attempted to harpoon the

dead pig in Allardyce's butcher shop. We know also that he was 'a bit of a single-stick expert,' while some of his early adventures among the medieval moats, turrets and drawbridges of the English aristocracy would naturally have attracted him to a study in military fortifications.

"Only in Japan," concluded Count Makino, "do we find one comprehensive science which includes all these studies. Only in Sherlock Holmes do we find a Westerner who combines a notable skill in all of them. For us Japanese there is intense satisfaction in the foundation of this first Tokyo chapter of the Baker Street Irregulars, under a name perpetuating that complex and subtle Japanese art which saved the hero of the West and of the East for further unforgettable adventures."

East and West

Other members of the Baritsu chapter include Edogawa Rampo (a pseudonym transliterated from Edgar Allan Poe), Japan's leading mystery writer; George F. Blewett, Philadelphia defence attorney for the late General Hideki Tojo; your own representative: and Walter Simmons, founder of the chapter, member of the parent Baker Street Irregulars and distinguished Far Eastern correspondent for Colonel McCormick's Chicago "Tribune," which, despite its frenetic anti-British policy, prints regularly the most graceful and erudite references to Holmes and Watson in Vincent Starrett's celebrated "Books Alive" column.

Truly Holmes — now in his ninety-sixth year and living in contented and immortal retirement among his Sussex beehives — has succeeded in bringing the East and the West together, irrespective of race, colour and political ideology. The philosophic observer may well speculate on the significance in current international affairs of the continued absence of any branch of the Baker Street Irregulars in Moscow and of the stubborn refusal of Joseph Stalin to read any of the Sherlock Holmes adventures.

An outstanding magazine cover featuring Sherlock Holmes. The artist for this issue of "Collier's" was Frederic Dorr Steele.

The Church Times May 1910

MISTAKEN FOR HOLMES!

In 1908 I travelled down the rivers Volga and Kama into Kazan. I had a job as tutor to the two sons of the Marshal of Nobility of that province.

I found all Russia crazy about Sherlock Holmes. Even the peasants (those who could read) had got hold of copies, cheaply printed and, no doubt, pirated. But evidently the Paget pictures had arrived, too, and they knew what he looked like.

This was evident when my two youngsters, seeing that I was tall, lean, clean-shaven and pipe-smoking, insisted that I was the living image of S.H. and begged that they might take me over to a nearby village and show me off as the genuine article!

I have always regretted that I did not undertake that hoax!

REVEREND GERALD HERRING, Parys Hotel, Parys, South Africa

The Apocryphal Sherlock Holmes The Adventure of the First Class Carriage

The general encouragement extended to my efforts by the public is my excuse, if excuse were needed, for continuing to act as chronicler of my friend Sherlock Holmes. But even if I confine myself to those cases in which I have had the honour of being personally associated with him, I find it difficult to make a selection among the large amount of matter at my disposal.

As I turn over my records, I find that some of them deal with events of national or even international importance; but the time has not yet come when it would be safe to disclose (for instance) the true facts about the recent change of government in Paraguay. Others (like the case of the Missing Omnibus) would do more to gratify the modern craving for sensation; but I am well aware that my friend himself is the first to deplore it when I indulge what is, in his own view, a weakness.

My preference is for recording incidents whose bizarre features gave special opportunity for the exercise of that analytical talent which he possessed in such a marked degree. Of these, the case of the Tattooed Nurseryman and that of the Luminous Cigar-Box naturally suggest themselves to the mind. But perhaps my friend's gifts were even more signally displayed when he had occasion to investigate the disappearance of Mr. Nathaniel Swithinbank, which provoked so much speculation in the early days of September, five years back.

Mr. Sherlock Holmes was, of all men, the least influenced by what are called class distinctions. To him the rank was but the guinea stamp; a client was a client. And it did not surprise me, one evening when I was sitting over the familiar fire in Baker Street — the days were sunny but the evenings were already falling chill — to be told that he was expecting a visit from a domestic servant, a woman who "did" for a well-to-do, childless couple in the southern Midlands. "My last visit," he explained, "was from a countess. Her mind was uninteresting, and she had no great regard for the truth; the problem she brought was quite elementary. I fancy Mrs. John Hennessy will have something more important to communicate."

"You have met her already, then?"

"No, I have not had the privilege. But anyone who is in the habit of receiving letters from strangers will tell you the same — handwriting is often a better form of introduction than hand-shaking. You will find Mrs. Hennessy's letter on the mantelpiece; and if you care to look at her j's and her w's, in particular, I think you will agree that it is no ordinary woman we have to deal with. Dear me, there is the bell ringing already; in a

moment or two, if I mistake not, we shall know what Mrs. Hennessy, of the Cottage, Guiseborough St. Martin, wants of Sherlock Holmes."

There was nothing in the appearance of the old dame who was shown up, a few minutes later, by the faithful Mrs. Hudson to justify Holmes's estimate. To the outward view she was a typical representative of her class; from the bugles on her bonnet to her elastic-sided boots everything suggested the old-fashioned caretaker such as you may see polishing the front doorsteps of a hundred office buildings any spring morning in the city of London. Her voice, when she spoke, was articulated with unnecessary care, as that of the respectable working-class woman is apt to be. But there was something precise and business-like about the statement of her case which made you feel that this was a mind which could easily have profited by greater educational advantages.

"I have read of you, Mr. Holmes," she began, "and when things began to go wrong up at the Hall it wasn't long before I thought to myself, If there's one man in England who will be able to see light here, it's Mr. Sherlock Holmes. My husband was in good employment, till lately, on the railway at Chester; but the time came when the rheumatism got hold of him, and after that nothing seemed to go well with us until he had thrown up his job, and we went to live in a country village not far from Banbury, looking out for any odd work that might come our way.

"We had only been living there a week when a Mr. Swithinbank and his wife took the old Hall, that had long been standing empty. They were newcomers to the district, and their needs were not great, having neither chick nor child to fend for; so they engaged me and Mr. Hennessy to come and live in the lodge, close by the house, and do all the work of it for them. The pay was good and the duties light, so we were glad enough to get the billet."

"One moment!" said Holmes. "Did they advertise, or were you indebted to some private recommendation for the appointment?"

"They came at short notice, Mr. Holmes, and were directed to us for temporary help. But they soon saw that our ways suited them, and they kept us on. They were people who kept very much to themselves, and perhaps they did not want a set of maids who would have followers, and spread gossip in the village."

This was the last Holmes story to be published in the "Strand" before its demise. Father Knox was perhaps the greatest of all Sherlockian experts.

Illustrated by Tom Purvis

"That is suggestive. You state your case with admirable clearness. Pray proceed."

"All this was no longer ago than last July. Since then they have once been away in London, but for the most part they have lived at Guiseborough, seeing very little of the folk round about. Parson called, but he is not a man to put his nose in where he is not wanted, and I think they must have made it clear they would sooner have his room than his company. So there was more guessing than gossiping about them in the country-side. But, sir, you can't be in domestic employment without finding out a good deal about how the land lies; and it wasn't long before my husband and I were certain of two things. One was that Mr. and Mrs. Swithinbank were deep in debt. And the other was that they got on badly together."

"Debts have a way of reflecting themselves in a man's correspondence," said Holmes, "and whoever has the clearing of his waste-paper basket will necessarily be conscious of them. But the relations between man and wife? Surely they must have gone very wrong indeed before there is quarrelling in public."

"That's as may be, Mr. Holmes, but quarrel in public they did. Why, it was only last week I came in with the blanc-mange, and he was saying, *The fact is, no one would be better pleased than you to see me in my coffin.* To be sure, he held his tongue after that, and looked a bit confused; and she tried to put a brave face on it. But I've lived long enough, Mr. Holmes, to know when a woman's been crying. Then last Monday, when I'd been in drawing the curtains, he burst out just before I'd closed the door behind me, *The world isn't big enough for both of us.* That was all I heard, and right glad I'd have been to hear less. But I've not come round here just to repeat servants'-hall gossip.

"To-day, when I was cleaning out the waste-paper basket, I came across a scrap of a letter that tells the same story, in his own handwriting. Cast your eye over that, Mr. Holmes, and tell me whether a Christian woman has the right to sit by and do nothing about it."

She had dived her hand into a capacious reticule and brought out, with a triumphant flourish, her documentary evidence. Holmes knitted his brow over it, and then passed it on to me. It ran: "Being of sound mind, whatever the numbskulls on the jury may say of it."

"Can you identify the writing?" my friend said.

"It was my master's," replied Mrs. Hennessy, "I know it well enough; the bank, I am sure, will tell you the same."

"Mrs. Hennessy, let us make no bones about it. Curiosity is a well-marked instinct of the human species. Your eye having lighted on this document, no doubt inadvertently, I will wager you took a look round the basket for any other fragments it might contain."

"That I did, sir; my husband and I went through it carefully together, for who knew but the life of a fellow-creature might depend on it? But only one other piece could we find written by the same hand, and on the same note-paper. Here it is." And she smoothed out on her knee a second fragment, to all appearances part of the same sheet, yet strangely different in its tenor. It seemed to have been torn away from the middle of a sentence; nothing survived but the words "in the reeds by the lake, taking a bearing at the point where the old tower hides both the middle first-floor windows."

"Come," I said, "this at least gives us something to go upon. Mrs. Hennessy will surely be able to tell us whether there are any landmarks in Guiseborough answering to this description."

"Indeed there are, sir; the directions are plain as a pikestaff. There is an old ruined building which juts out upon the little lake at the bottom of the garden, and it would be easy enough to hit on the place mentioned. I daresay you gentlemen are wondering why we haven't been down to the lake-side ourselves to see what we could find there. Well, the plain fact is, we were scared. My master is a quiet-spoken man enough at ordinary times, but there's a wild look in his eye when he's roused, and I for one should be sorry to cross him. So I thought I'd come to you, Mr. Holmes, and put the whole thing in your hands."

"I shall be interested to look into your little difficulty. To speak frankly, Mrs. Hennessy, the story you have told me runs on such familiar lines that I should have been tempted to dismiss the whole case from my mind. Dr. Watson here will tell you that I am a busy man, and the affairs of the Bank of Mauritius urgently require my presence in London. But this last detail about the reeds by the lake-side is piquant, decidely piquant, and the whole matter shall be gone into. The only difficulty is a practical one. How are we to explain my presence at Guiseborough without betraying to your employers the fact that you and your husband have been intruding on their family affairs?"

"I have thought of that, sir," replied the old dame, "and I think we can find a way out. I slipped away to-day easily enough because my mistress is going abroad to visit her aunt, near Dieppe, and Mr. Swithinbank has come up to Town with her to see her off. I must go back by the evening train, and had half thought of asking you to accompany me. But no, he would get to hear of it if a stranger visited the place in his absence. It would be better if you came down by the quarter-past ten train to-morrow, and passed yourself off for a stranger who was coming to look at the house. They have taken it on a short lease, and plenty of folks come to see it without troubling to obtain an order-to-view."

Will your employer be back so early?"

"That is the very train he means to take; and to speak truth, sir, I should be the better for knowing that he was being watched. This wicked talk of making away with himself is enough to make anyone anxious about him. You cannot mistake him, Mr. Holmes," she went on; "what chiefly marks him out is a scar on the left-hand side of his chin, where a dog bit him when he was a youngster."

"Excellent, Mrs. Hennessy; you have thought of everything. To-morrow, then, on the quarter-past ten for Banbury without fail. You will oblige me by ordering the station fly to be in readiness. Country walks may be good for health, but time is more

precious. I will drive straight to your cottage, and you or your husband shall escort me on my visit to this desirable country residence and its mysterious tenant." With a wave of his hand, he cut short her protestations of gratitude.

"Well, Watson, what did you make of her?" asked my companion when the door had closed on our visitor.

"She seemed typical of that noble army of women whose hard scrubbing makes life easy for the leisured classes. I could not see her well because she sat between us and the window, and her veil was lowered over her eyes. But her manner was enough to convince me that she was telling us the truth, and that she is sincere in her anxiety to avert what may be an appalling tragedy. As to its nature, I confess I am in the dark. Like yourself, I was particularly struck by the reference to the reeds by the lake-side. What can it mean? An assignation?"

"Hardly, my dear Watson. At this time of the year a man runs enough risk of cold without standing about in a reed-bed. A hiding-place, more probably, but for what? And why should a man take the trouble to hide something, and then obligingly litter his waste-paper basket with clues to its whereabouts? No, these are deep waters, Watson, and we must have more data before we begin to theorise. You will come with me?"

"Certainly, if I may. Shall I bring my revolver?"

"I do not apprehend any danger, but perhaps it is as well to be on the safe side. Mr. Swithinbank seems to strike his neighbours as a formidable person. And now, if you will be good enough to hand me the more peaceful instrument which hangs beside you, I will try out that air of Scarlatti's, and leave the affairs of Guiseborough St. Martin to look after themselves."

I often had occasion to deprecate Sherlock Holmes's habit of catching trains with just half a minute to spare. But on the morning after our interview with Mrs. Hennessy we arrived at Paddington station no later than ten o'clock — to find a stranger, with a pronounced scar on the left side of his chin, gazing out at us languidly from the window of a first-class carriage.

"Do you mean to travel with him?" I asked, when we were out of earshot.

"Scarcely feasible, I think. If he is the man I take him for, he has secured solitude all the way to Banbury by the simple process of slipping half a crown into the guard's hand." And, sure enough, a few minutes later we saw that functionary shepherd a fussy-looking gentleman, who had been vigorously assaulting the locked door, to a compartment farther on. For ourselves, we took up our post in the carriage next but one behind Mr. Swithinbank. This, like the other first-class compartments, was duly locked when we had entered it; behind us the less fortunate passengers accommodated themselves in seconds.

The case is not without its interest," observed Holmes, laying down his paper as we steamed through Burnham Beeches. "It presents features which recall the affairs of James Phillimore, whose disappearance (though your loyalty may tempt you to forget it) we investigated without success. But this Swithinbank mystery, if I mistake not, cuts even deeper. Why, for

example, is the man so anxious to parade his intention of suicide, or fictitious suicide, in the presence of his domestic staff? It can hardly fail to strike you that he chose the moment when the good Mrs. Hennessy was just entering the room, or just leaving it, to make those remarkable confidences to his wife. Not content with that, he must leave evidence of his intentions lying about in the waste-paper basket. And yet this involved the risk of having his plans foiled by good-natured interference. Time enough for his disappearance to become public when it became effective! And why, in the name of fortune, does he hide something only to tell us where he has hidden it?"

Amid a maze of railway-tracks, we came to a standstill at Reading. Holmes craned his neck out of the window, but reported that all the doors had been left locked. We were not destined to learn anything about our elusive travelling-companion until, just as we were passing the pretty hamlet of Tilehurst, a little shower of paper fragments fluttered past the window on the right-hand side of the compartment, and two of them actually sailed in through the space we had dedicated to ventilation on that bright morning of autumn. It may easily be guessed with what avidity we had pounced on them.

The messages were in the same handwriting with which Mrs. Hennessy's find had made us familiar; they ran, respectively, "Mean to make an end of it all" and "This is the only way out." Holmes sat over them with knitted brows, till I fairly danced with impatience.

"Should we not pull the communication-cord?" I asked.

"Hardly," answered my companion, "unless five-pound notes are more plentiful with you than they used to be. I will even anticipate your next suggestion, which is that we should look out of the windows on either side of the carriage. Either we have a lunatic two doors off, in which case there is no use in trying to foresee his next move, or he intends suicide, in which case he will not be deterred by the presence of spectators, or he is a man with a scheming brain who is sending us these messages in order to make us behave in a particular way. Quite possibly, he wants to make us lean out of the windows, which seems to me an excellent reason for not leaning out of the windows. At Oxford we shall be able to read the guard a lesson on the danger of locking passengers in."

So indeed it proved; for when the train stopped at Oxford there was no passenger to be found in Mr. Swithinbank's carriage. His overcoat remained, and his wide-brimmed hat; his portmanteau was duly identified in the guard's van. The door on the right-hand side of the compartment, away from the platform, had not swung open; nor did Holmes's lens bring to light any details about the way in which the elusive passenger had made his exit.

It was an impatient horse and an injured cabman that awaited us at Banbury, when we drove through golden woodlands to the little village of Guiseborough St. Martin, nestling under the shadow of Edge Hill. Mrs. Hennessy met us at the door of her cottage, dropping an old-fashioned curtsy; and it may easily be imagined what wringing of hands, what wiping of eyes with her apron, greeted the announcement of her

master's disappearance. Mr. Hennessy, it seemed, had gone off to a neighbouring farm upon some errand, and it was the old dame herself who escorted us up to the Hall.

"There's a gentleman there already, Mr. Holmes," she informed us. "Arrived early this morning and would take no denial; and not a word to say what business he came on."

"That is unfortunate," said Holmes. "I particularly wanted a free field to make some investigations. Let us hope that he will be good enough to clear off when he is told that there is no chance of an interview with Mr. Swithinbank."

Guiseborough Hall stands in its own grounds a little way outside the village, the residence of a squire unmistakably, but with no airs of baronial grandeur. The old, rough walls have been refaced with pointed stone, the mullioned windows exchanged for a generous expanse of plate-glass, to suit a more recent taste, and a portico has been thrown out from the front door to welcome the traveller with its shelter. The garden descends at a precipitous slope from the main terrace, and a little lake fringes it at the bottom, dominated by a ruined eminence that serves the modern owner for a gazebo.

Within the house, furniture was of the scantiest, the Swithinbanks having evidently rented it with what fittings it had, and introduced little of their own. As Mrs. Hennessy ushered us into the drawing-room, we were not a little surprised to be greeted by the wiry figure and melancholy features of our old rival, Inspector Lestrade.

"I knew you were quick off the mark, Mr. Holmes," he said, "but it beats me how you ever heard of Mr. Swithinbank's little goings-on; let alone that I didn't think you took much stock in cases of common fraud like this."

"Common fraud?" repeated my companion. "Why, what has he been up to?"

"Drawing cheques, and big ones, Mr. Holmes, when he knew that his bank wouldn't honour them; only little things of that sort. But if you're on his track I don't suppose he's far off, and I'll be grateful for any help you can give me to lay my hands on him."

"My dear Lestrade, if you follow out your usual systematic methods, you will have to patrol the Great Western Line all the way from Reading to Oxford. I trust you have brought a drag-net with you, for the line crossed the river no less than four times in the course of the journey." And he regaled the astonished inspector with a brief summary of our investigations.

Our information worked like a charm on the little detective. He was off in a moment to find the nearest telegraph office and put himself in touch with Scotland Yard, with the Great Western Railway authorities, with the Thames Conservancy. He promised, however, a speedy return, and I fancy Holmes cursed himself for not having dismissed the jarvey who had brought us from the station, an undeserved windfall for our rival.

"Now Watson!" he cried as the sound of the wheels faded away into the distance.

"Our way lies to the lake-side, I presume."

"How often am I to remind you that the place

where the criminal tells you to look is the place not to look? No, the clue to the mystery lies, somehow, in the house, and we must hurry up if we are to find it."

Quick as a thought, he began turning out shelves, cupboards, escritoires, while I, at his direction, went through the various rooms of the house to ascertain whether all was in order, and whether anything suggested the anticipation of a hasty flight. By the time I returned to him, having found nothing amiss, he was seated in the most comfortable of the drawing-room armchairs, reading a book he had picked out of the shelves — it dealt, if I remember right, with the aborigines of Borneo.

"The mystery, Holmes!" I cried.

"I have solved it. If you will look on the bureau yonder, you will find the household books which Mrs. Swithinbank has obligingly left behind. Extraordinary how these people always make some elementary mistake. You are a man of the world, Watson; take a look at them and tell me what strikes you as curious."

It was not long before the salient feature occurred to me. "Why, Holmes," I exclaimed, "there is no record of the Hennessys being paid any wages at all!"

"Bravo, Watson! And if you will go into the figures a little more closely, you will find that the Hennessys apparently lived on air. So now the whole facts of the story are plain to you."

"I confess," I replied, somewhat crestfallen, "that the whole case is as dark to me as ever."

"Why, then, take a look at that newspaper I have left on the occasional table; I have marked the important paragraph in blue pencil."

It was a copy of an Australian paper, issued some weeks previously. The paragraph to which Holmes had drawn my attention ran thus:

Romance of rich man's will

The recent lamented death of Mr. John Macready, the well-known sheep-farming magnate, has had an unexpected sequel in the circumstance that the dead man, apparently, left no will. His son, Mr. Alexander Macready, left for England some years back, owing to a misunderstanding with his father — it was said — because he announced his intention of marrying a lady from the stage. The young man has completely disappeared, and energetic steps are being taken by the lawyers to trace his whereabouts. It is estimated that the fortunate heirs, whoever they be, will be the richer by not far short of a hundred thousand pounds sterling.

Horse-hoofs echoed under the archway, and in another minute Lestrade was again of our party. Seldom have I seen the little detective looking so baffled and ill at ease. "They'll have the laugh of me at the Yard over this," he said. "We had word that Swithinbank was in London, but I made sure it was only a feint, and I came racing up here by the early train, instead of catching the quarter-past ten and my man in it. He's a slippery devil, and he may be half-way to the Continent by this time."

"Don't be down-hearted about it, Lestrade. Come and interview Mr. and Mrs. Hennessy, at the lodge; we may get news of your man down there."

A coarse-looking fellow in a bushy red beard sat sharing his tea with our friend of the evening before. His greasy waistcoat and corduroy trousers proclaimed him a manual worker. He rose to meet us with something of a defiant air; his wife was all affability.

"Have you heard any news of the poor 'gentleman?" she asked.

"We may have some before long," answered Holmes. "Lestrade, you might arrest John Hennessy for stealing that porter's cap you see on the dresser, the property of the Great Western Railway Company. Or, if you prefer an alternative charge, you might arrest him as Alexander Macready, *alias* Nathaniel Swithinbank." And while we stood there literally thunder-struck, he tore off the red beard from a chin marked with a scar on the left-hand side.

"The case was difficult," he said to me afterwards, "only because we had no clue to the motive. Swithinbank's debts would almost have swallowed up Macready's legacy; it was necessary for the couple to disappear, and take up the claim under a fresh *alias*. This meant a duplication of personalities, but it was not really difficult. She had been an actress; he had really been a railway porter in his hard-up days. When he got out at Reading, and passed along the six-foot way to take his place in a third-class carriage, nobody marked the circumstance, because on the way from London he had changed into a porter's clothes; he had the cap, no doubt, in his pocket. On the sill of the door he left open, he had made a little pile of suicide-messages, hoping that when it swung open these would be shaken out and flutter into the carriages behind."

"But why the visit to London? And, above all, why the visit to Baker Street?"

"That is the most amusing part of the story; we should have seen through it at once. He wanted Nathaniel Swithinbank to disappear finally, beyond all hope of tracing him. And who would hope to trace him, when Mr. Sherlock Holmes, who was travelling only two carriages behind, had given up the attempt? Their only fear was that I should find the case uninteresting; hence the random reference to a hiding-place among the reeds, which so intrigued you. Come to think of it, they nearly had Inspector Lestrade in the same train as well. I hear he has won golden opinions with his superiors by cornering his man so neatly. *Sic vos non vobis,* as Virgil said of the bees; only they tell us nowadays the lines are not by Virgil."

John O'London's March 26 1954

THE FINAL PROBLEM

Some years ago I read the life of that once best-selling author, Silas K. Hocking (1850-1935), in which he described a holiday sight-seeing in Switzerland shared by his friend Dr. Conan Doyle, when the latter confessed he would finally like to dispose of Sherlock Holmes; to which Silas Hocking replied that there and then he had a most excellent and dramatic opportunity of doing so, by dropping him down the abyss into the raging torrent at the bottom of the Reichenbach Falls.

This is the only mention I have come across as to how the plot for Holmes' supposed death originated.

Louisa L. Richardson,
Kitale, Kenya.

The Motor August 27 1952

Deer-stalker, Deasy and All

Sherlock Holmes used to "hail a hansom" when he was in a hurry, often taking Watson with him; he did not "keep a carriage". I often wonder whether, had he lived somewhat later, Holmes would have driven a car himself; somehow I do not think he would.

Dr. Watson, of course, would quickly have succumbe to the "new locomotion" and bought himself a De Dior on the recommendation of a colleague, a used one, in somewhat questionable condition, which Holmes would be apt to scorn.

"Thank you," I picture him saying. "But time presse 'The Case of the Missing Cylinder' is one which we may well leave to our good friend Inspector Lestrade."

Holmes himself would have hired, when motoring became a necessity, from the father of one of his Baker Street Irregulars who had set up a garage in Marylebone a Siddeley-Deasy, perhaps. It would go so well with his hat.

"King-Pin"

Footnote: Sherlock Holmes only once travelled by car during all his adventures, when he emerged from retirement during World War I to serve in "His Last Bow" (1917), and then Dr. Watson was the driver!

'Museum Robbery . . . Home Guard Revival . . . Elementary, My Dear Watson!'

The Great Detective in caricature: Moon cartoon from "The Sunday Dispatch" of November 1950; Hewison providing transport for Holmes and Watson in "Punch" in 1953.

The Times October 27 1950

Case against Sherlock Holmes

Councillors of St. Marylebone have opposed a suggestion by the borough library committee for a Sherlock Holmes exhibition in the public library as a contribution to the Festival of Britain. Councillor Tom Vernon (Lab.) said: "It would be more constructive to show the world the great progress this borough has made in clearing away the noxious slums of 100 years ago." Alderman F. W. Dean (Con.) leader of the council said for once he agreed with the other side: St. Marylebone had "many things to show off about without Sherlock Holmes."

Holmes congratulating his sometime associate, Inspector Lestrade, in "The Adventure of the Norwood Builder" (1903).

The Times October 28 1950

The curious case of Sherlock Holmes

Sir.— It is doubtful whether Mr. Sherlock Holmes will have seen the paragraph in THE TIMES to-day recording the singular decision of the councillors of St. Marylebone to oppose the proposal for an exhibition of *materiae* of my old friend and mentor for the benefit of visitors to the Festival of Britain. Engrossed as he is in bee-keeping in Sussex, he is unlikely to rally to his own defence, and you will perhaps allow me, as a humble chronicler of some of his cases and as a former resident in the borough, to express indignation at this decision.

There is much housing in the Metropolis but there is but one Mr. Sherlock Holmes, and I venture to assert that visitors from across the Atlantic (who cannot as yet have forgotten my old friend's remarkable work in clearing up the dark mystery of the Valley of Fear in the grotesque affair of the Study in Scarlet) would find such an exhibition of interest. Why the councillors of St. Marylebone, in their anxiety to display their work on the clearing of slums, should deny honour to my old friend I find it hard to understand. Perhaps this is time's revenge for the exposure of Mr. Sherlock Holmes for the evil machinations of the Norwood Builder. Whatever the reason, I trust that second and better thoughts may prevail, and in the meantime subscribe myself,

Your humble but indignant servant, JOHN H. WATSON, M.D. late of the Indian Army.
October 27

The Times November 2 1950

Holmes and his "gifted guesswork"

Sir.— Long years of retirement have failed to break the professional habit of careful examination of the Personal columns of *The Times* newspaper and a necessarily hastier perusal of its other contents. Thus I have learned with no little surprise of the proposal to stage an exhibition perpetuating the performances of my old acquaintance, Mr. Sherlock Holmes. Surely in this correspondence to-day's letter from Mrs. Hudson, his worthy landlady, places the abilities of Mr. Holmes in their right perspective. A place of amusement, such as Madame Tussaud's, is surely the proper setting for a record of Holmes's amateur achievements. It would be ungenerous of me to deny that on occasion the gifted guesswork of Mr. Holmes has jumped a stage in the final solution of a crime. It may not be inappropriate to remind your readers, however, of the fable of the tortoise and the hare, and the true student of criminology will continue to regard as the only true source the so-called "Black Museum" of that institution on the Victoria Embankment which for so many years I had the honour to serve.

G. LESTRADE, ex-Inspector, Metropolitan Police, Laburnum Road, Tooting, S.W.,

"But how did you know young Bromley murdered the haberdasher, Holmes?"

Holmes: Very simple, my dear Watson. Young Bromley is known as a fanatic fashion plate. And yet there he stood, protesting his innocence, in a shirt that fitted him badly all around.

Watson: *Of course, Holmes. Young Bromley always wears ARROW shirts. Perfect style at the collar. Exact sleeve length. "Sanforized". Tapered ARROW fit.*

Holmes: Quite so. Obviously our haberdasher had talked Bromley into trying a different shirt. It fitted atrociously. And in a rage, Bromley struck him down.

Bromley: *He told me it was an ARROW. He told me....*

Holmes: Poor devil. I can't help but believe there was strong provocation, Watson.

ARROW
The shirt for Britain—*with a dash of American*

"SANFORIZED" FABRICS. Available in regular and drip-dry finishes.
Prices range from 32/6.

CLUETT, PEABODY & CO., LTD., 24 NEW BOND STREET, LONDON W.1
Holmes and Watson appear by agreement with Trustee of the Estate of Sir Arthur Conan Doyle

1959

The interior of 221B Baker Street as it was designed by Michael Wright in 1951 for the Festival of Britain.

A HOLMES EXHIBITION FOR FESTIVAL
Doubts removed in St. Marylebone

A sense of relief will be spread in surprisingly wide circles by the news that last night's meeting of the library committee of St. Marylebone confirmed its proposal to hold a Sherlock Holmes exhibition during the Festival of Britain next year.

Nor is there any reason to fear that the project will encounter further criticism in the borough council. There seems, indeed, to have been a little misunderstanding about the significance of some observations that Mr. T. Vernon felt moved to offer in the council meeting last Thursday. His explanation of his attitude in *The Times* yesterday is in harmony with the statement made after last night's meeting of the library committee by Miss L. F. Nettlefold, its chairman. She pointed out that the proposal was accepted by the borough council on Thursday and would now go forward.

The exhibition will be held in the St. Marylebone public library. If anyone doubts whether material exists for such a commemoration in the unaccountable absence of authentic relics of the great detective, the answer is that there is a great deal. Much literary material is already in the library itself, and a rich store of informed enthusiasm waits to be drawn upon among the library staff. It is, of course, one of the chief glories of Marylebone that Holmes had lodgings for many years at 221B, Baker Street. It may be less commonly known that Conan Doyle, his chronicler, lived at 2, Devonshire Street.

It is too early to indicate the scope of the exhibition, but there are possibilities enough. Hundreds of articles and dozens of books have been published on Sherlock Holmes and Dr. Watson. There is a scholarly bibliography of books about them. A selection from these will doubtless be included in the exhibition. It may well contain records of the lives of Conan Doyle and Dr. Joseph Bell, under whom Doyle studied medicine and who is said to have shared many of the traits of Sherlock Holmes. It is hoped to have on view original manuscripts of some of the stories, and perhaps to borrow (if it still exists) a leaf of a notebook on which was set out the original idea of *A Study in Scarlet*, with the detective misnamed, regrettably, Sherinford Holmes.

Records and minutes of the various Sherlock Holmes societies might be assembled.

America, incidentally, more than makes up for the relative scarcity of British societies. The Marylebone library files the journal of the Baker Street Irregulars of America. This records the names of "scion societies" and their progress. Most of them set exceedingly stiff examination papers for would-be members, and some specimens would be an interesting addition to the exhibition. Some of their names deserve to be mentioned. — "The Seventeen Steps of Los Angeles," "The Speckled Band of Boston," "The Scandalous Bohemians of Akron," "The Amateur Mendicant Society of Detroit," "The Dancing Men of Providence," "The Canadian Baskervilles," and "The Illustrious Clients of Indianapolis." One must not forget the society known as "The Solitary Cyclist of Washington, D.C.," consisting of one (woman) member.

Sherlock Holmes's Deerstalker

As the daughter of Sidney Paget, the illustrator of 'Sherlock Holmes' in the Strand Magazine, I was very interested to read your article entitled 'The Return of Sherlock Holmes' and think perhaps some of your readers might be interested to know what became of the famous deerstalker hat.

My father lived in the country and like most artists, followed many pursuits, but I do not think that deer-stalking was one of them! I imagine that he chose this type of hat for himself as being suitable and comfortable for tramping round the countryside, which fact possibly inspired him to depict Holmes wearing a deerstalker on similar occasions. It seems to me to be a fitting headgear for the great detective out on the man-hunt! Little did my father know that this hat would still be talked about half a century after it first appeared in the pages of the Strand.

Many years after my father's death, at the early age of 47, the deerstalker was savagely attacked by moths who apparently are no respecters of ancient relics and reluctantly my mother consigned it to the dustbin, so I fear there is an empty peg beside that on which one hopes Watson's bowler still hangs on 221B Baker Street, unless, this too has suffered the same fate!

WINIFRED PAGET,
Oxhey Road, Watford.

men only

MAY

1951

PRICE

1/6

NET

HYNES.

SHERLOCK HOLMES

Not so elementary, my dear Watson

Date	NAME	ADDRESS	REMARKS
1915.			
July 3	Nathanie Lawson	Ardington	Church Bleau
8	C. A. Weston	Endon, Staffs.	
July 11	Nellie Gwinnell (leading lady of the Dandy Fifth Coy)	London E. Christ-Church	Much touched by beautiful window
July 13	Conan Doyle. (Novelist).		Have thought out a Sherlock Holmes story here.
July 13	Hywel Davies.	Nantgaredig.	Window beautiful
July		Suffolk.	

A mystery worthy of the attention of Sherlock Holmes himself has developed in Shrewsbury — around the affairs of Sir Arthur Conan Doyle.

The Rev. Sidney Austerberry, rector of St. Alkmund's Church, has found a visitors' book for 1915. Beneath an entry by "Nellie Gwinnell" — itself a name to conjure with — who describes herself as "leading lady of the Dandy Fifth Company" and who was "much touched by the beautiful window," appears, against the date July 13, the signature "Conan Doyle (novelist)" and the note: "Have thought out a Sherlock Holmes story here."

Seeking confirmation that the signature is genuine, Mr. J. L. Hobbs, Shrewsbury librarian, turned up newspaper files in an attempt to discover whether the novelist was in Shrewsbury at this time.

He was unable to do so — but Miss A. E. Corbett, of Coton Crescent, Shrewsbury, was able to confirm that on March 13 the same year she was taken to a literary society meeting in the town to hear the novelist speak.

Afterwards, she asked for — and was given — his autograph, which she still preserves.

After comparing the autograph with the signature in the visitors' book, Mr. Hobbs is satisfied that they were not written by the same person.

The two specimens are "quite different," and the signature Sir Arthur gave Corbett reads: "*Arthur Conan Doyle.*"

Holmes and Watson studying a clue in "The Problem of Thor Bridge" by another of the later "Strand Magazine" illustrators, A. Gilbert (1922).

The Times October 31 1950

OH, NO JOHN (WATSON), NO!

When I called on Dr. Watson for his help in the search for my husband (you will remember the un-paralleled horror of the denouement in the Case of the Man with the Twisted Lip) I distinctly heard his wife address him as James. It is, therefore, with no little perturbation and distress that I read in today's issue of *The Times* a letter purporting to have been written by the good doctor and signed by the obviously fictitious name of John.

KATE WHITNEY,
London.

The Times November 1 1950

THE ACHIEVEMENTS OF MY LODGER

As I am still a ratepayer in the Borough of St. Marylebone, may I suggest that the obvious place for an exhibition devoted to the achievements of my former lodger, Mr. Sherlock Holmes, is Madam Tussaud's, whose premises are situated only a few yards from my house and are also, of course, in the Borough of St. Marylebone.

They could take this opportunity of rectifying a long-standing omission by placing models of Mr. Holmes and Dr. Watson upstairs, and of many of the criminals whom Mr. Holmes arrested, downstairs. For many years I have been a regular visitor to Madame Tussaud's, but I have never yet noticed Professor Moriarty, Dr. Grimesby Roylott, "Mr. Stapleton", or any of the others in that famous basement. American

visitors would naturally be pleased to see Abe Slaney too.

Naturally, gruesome relics will be required. Dr. Watson has several which Mr. Holmes gave him (Including Mr. Culverton Smith's black and white ivory box), and I expect Mr. Holmes still has that large tin box full of papers and souvenirs. Perhaps the present Duke of Holdernesse could be prevailed upon to lend his set of cow-like horses' shoes, and I will lend the wax bust of Mr. Holmes which Monsieur Oscar Meunier made and Colonel Moran spoilt with an airgun bullet.

Please forgive an uneducated person writing to so important a newspaper as *The Times*.

MRS. HUDSON
221B, Baker Street, W.1.

The Times November 4 1950

HOLMES AND THE OCCULT

I read Mrs. Hudson's letter with great interest, and I think I am in a position to give you information which has an important bearing upon her suggestion.

Your readers may not know that at the time I made the wax bust of Mr. Holmes I was in the employ of Madame Tussaud and Sons Limited. Holmes gave me many sittings so that I could obtain a perfect like-ness and, like so many people with whom he came into contact, I was entranced by his powers as a conversationalist.

As we are well aware, his know-ledge of the occult, and particularly the practice of the black arts, was phenomenal. Quite naturally, we discussed at considerable length the use of wax figures in image magic, and it did not come as a surprise to me to learn that he was disinclined

to dismiss their effectiveness in certain circumstances. On the con-trary, he held very strong beliefs on the subject, and when I had com-pleted the wax bust to his entire satisfaction he asked me to ensure that at no time should a wax portrait of himself be placed on display.

Although Holmes has now retired and is devoting his life to the study of bees, I am quite cer-tain that he would still oppose any suggestion that he, Dr. Watson, or indeed any of the men he brought to justice should be perpetrated by waxen images which he held in such distrust.

OSCAR MEUNIER
late of Grenoble.
Curthwaite Gardens, Enfield.

A HOLMES EXPERIMENT – I

Sir.– St. Marylebone Borough Council is arranging a Sherlock Holmes Exhibition as a contribution to the Festival of Britain. The exhibition will include a section dealing with some of the scientific aspects of Holmes's work, and we are anxious to illustrate, if possible, what appears to have been one of his more important investigations. Unfortunately, Watson was not himself particularly interested in chemistry, and we have failed to reconstruct the experiment from the meagre data provided. The relevant passage (from "The Naval Treaty," dated by Bell as 1888) is as follows:

A large curved retort was boiling furiously in the bluish flame of a Bunsen burner, and the distilled drops were condensing into a two-litre measure . . . He dipped into this bottle or that, drawing out a few drops of each with his glass pipette, and finally brought a test-tube containing a solution over to the table. In his right hand he had a slip of litmus-paper.

"You come at a crisis, Watson," said he, "If this paper remains blue, all is well. If it turns red, it means a man's life." He dipped it into the test-tube, and it flushed at once into a dull, dirty crimson . . . He turned to his desk and scribbled off several telegrams. . . . "A very commonplace little murder," said he.

We should be grateful if any reader could suggest what precisely this experiment can have been; any solution should be chemically sound, and of such a nature that it would enable Holmes to deduce that a murder had been committed.

GEOFFREY B. STEPHENS,
Borough Librarian,
St. Marylebone, N.W.1.

A HOLMES EXPERIMENT – II

Sir.– I well remember Sherlock telling me that in 1888 he had had the only case then on record of poisoning by methyl cyanide. This substance was not a scheduled poison in the Pharmacy Act of 1868, nor is it today. Nevertheless, it was effective in this case, which was an ordinary affair of a workman in a chemical factory who abstracted the poison to do away with a wife he could no longer tolerate. The man put a large dose of acetonitrile in a cup of tea and somehow induced her to drink it quickly. A director of the manufacturing firm, who had been up at Cambridge with my brother, asked for his help when the husband was suspected. The police allowed Sherlock to examine the viscera.

My brother soon identified the poison. His final confirmatory test is as well described by Watson as could be expected. Sherlock used a retort for the hydrolysis of the nitrile and for the distillation of the product, as there was no water supply in the sitting-room and no sink. He used dilute sulphuric acid for the hydrolysis, but the two-litre measure was *faute de mieux*. Since he was using a retort, there was some possibility of the sulphuric acid splashing over, and he accordingly tested a separate portion of the distillate for sulphate; but his technique of dipping a pipette into the hydrochloric acid and barium chloride reagent bottles was not ideal. When he knew that the distillate was free from sulphuric acid he relied on litmus to show the presence of acetic acid. The small amount of acid he obtained turned the litmus a dull, dirty crimson. This provided the confirmation of his chain of deductions and he was able to proceed with the apprehension of the criminal.

MYCROFT HOLMES,
Diogenes Club, S.W.1.

A HOLMES EXPERIMENT – III

Sir.– With reference to "The Adventure of the Red Litmus Paper" (Mr. Sherlock Holmes's experiment in the Naval Treaty Case):

Forty years ago we discussed this notorious experiment during the lunch interval in Professor Dixon's laboratory at Cambridge. (Dixon from internal evidence, was "the most distinguished pharmacologist" to whom A. E. W. Mason makes acknowledgement in the preface to the collected Hanaud stories.)

We were driven to the conclusion either that the Master had discovered some oriental drug unknown to science that could be detected by acidity of the distillate (a proposition abhorrent to any good addict of detection) or that he was pulling Dr. Watson's leg.

The suggestion that Dr. Watson invented the incident is made unlikely by a corroborative detail. Holmes sent off several telegrams. We know that the month was July, and those telegrams no doubt referred to bets on the coming Goodwood meeting. Holmes probably kept these activities quiet from Watson — especially after the "Silver Blaze" affair, for which he was lucky not have been warned off the Turf for life!

F. W. WATKYN-THOMAS,
United University Club.

A HOLMES EXPERIMENT – IV

Sir.– My attention has been directed to Mycroft's unnecessarily detailed account of a case Holmes never considered worthy of describing to me. I cannot accept the implied criticism of Holmes's methods.

It is absurd to suppose that the author of the Holmes haemoglobin reaction, and one whose name will always be associated with research into the coal-tar derivatives and analysis of the acetones, would be faulty in his elementary technique. As Mycroft must well know, what has happened here is that the printer or (just possibly, perhaps) my own notes carelessly omitted the s of pipettes.

Holmes would certainly not risk contaminating his reagents in this way when so often — as in this case — "it means a man's life."

J. H. WATSON,
Queen Anne Street, W.1.

BAKER STREET REVISITED
BY SHERLOCK HOLMES
(In an interview with HENRY LONGHURST)

I should be obliged if, through the medium of your admirable journal, I might express my appreciation of the St. Marylebone Borough Council's assistance to me in laying open to the public, in common with owners of other premises of historic interest, the chambers so long occupied by Dr. John H. Watson and myself in Baker Street.

The rooms, together with my papers, had as usual, through the supervision of my brother Mycroft and the immediate care of Mrs. Hudson, been preserved unchanged during my retirement. Only an unwonted tidiness betrayed my own long absence. How long this absence had indeed lasted was brought home to me on hearing a newspaper photographer inquire which of the items were "real" — that is, had in fact belonged to me!

The familiar interior, together with the yellow fog swirling outside our windows — almost obscuring the plaque to the actress, Mrs. Sarah Siddons, on the wall opposite, which Watson failed to notice in thirty years — the street cries, the clip-clop of the horses' hooves, and the itinerant musician still repeating the same discordant song almost as though on a gramophone record, all sent my mind racing back to what has well been called "a world where it is always 1895."

Those were, we are now assured, the bad old days. That they were more violent days I was reminded as my eye fell again on the harpoon in the corner (I wonder whether Allardyce's would have a whole pig for me to practise upon nowadays?), the knuckle-dusters and handcuffs, Colonel Moran's bullet-mark beside the door, to say nothing of the V R I so light-heartedly shot in the wall, and all the miscellaneous firearms, including not only Von Herder's celebrated airgun but also the superb gold-damascened Adams muzzle-loading revolver presented by the Duke of Montrose, for my services in a matter which His Grace may yet permit Watson to lay one day before the public.

I have been particularly happy to receive messages of good will from the Baker Street Irregulars in the United States and as their patron, I return greetings both to them and to such scion societies as the Musgrave Ritualists of New York, the Dancing Men of Providence, the Speckled Band of Boston and the Hounds of the Baskerville in Chicago.

It is always a joy to me to meet an American, as I told Mr. Francis Hay Moulton, and I continue to believe, sir, that the folly of a Monarch and the blundering of a Minister in fargone years will not prevent our children from being some day citizens of the same world-wide country.

As certain members of the public have during the past week addressed problems to me at Baker Street, may I add that advancing years — I will not say advanced, for I am only seven years senior to Dean Inge, who preached such an excellent sermon at Oxford only two Sundays ago — advancing years

keep me in retirement in Sussex, where, as President of the British Beekeepers' Association, I apply to apiarian problems the same great powers which I so long turned to the detection of crime.

Though I did, it is true, emerge from seclusion during the recent hostilities to assist the department now known as MI5, this was only on occasions when Mycroft had convinced me that continued failure on their part would imperil the entire outcome of the war. In peacetime my retirement remains complete.

I do not, of course, rate as an exception the not unexpected visit of an agitated successor of Lestrade's in connection with the, to him, mysterious episode in Westminster Abbey — partly because I was able in any case to set him upon the track without leaving my villa and partly because, as I more than once told Lestrade himself, I care only to be associated with those cases which present some little difficulty in their solution.

The Tatler and Bystander August 8 1951

THE SECRET WATSON
BY D. B. WYNDHAM LEWIS

One trusts that the Sherlock Holmes Society of London, just formed to "encourage the pursuit of knowledge of the public and private lives of Holmes and Watson," will devote especial attention to the last phase of the career of Watson, of which only the more sinister facts are known.

It was in 1904 that Watson was struck off the medical register. At the Old Bailey in 1905 his daughter Dinty deposed that he stopped drinking heavily and his practice picked up a little soon after Holmes was thrown off the Reichenbach by Moriarty. "Papa seemed a new man," said Miss Dinty Watson. "Unfortunately that so-and-so turned up again later, and Papa was soon the stooge as per usual. Mumsie was heartbroken. Of course we never dreamed, till after Mrs. Scattermole's dinner-party, that Papa was a lycanthrope."

The argument between the Astronomer-Royal and the Hyde Park keeper as to whether the moon was full or "gibbous" at the time when the women were mangled in the Park by Watson, then in wolf-shape, led to a severe rebuke for the keeper by the judge, if you remember.

His Lordship: This well-groomed gentleman (the Astronomer-Royal) gets £1500 a year for knowing about the moon, which is sucks-boo to you, I think? — I don't care, I got my job to do.

His Lordship: When you saw what looked like a wolf mangling these women, what did you do? — I shouted "Hoi! Stop that!"

His Lordship: You took no further action? — I got my job to do. I was picking up orange-peel. I got to keep my grass tidy.

His Lordship: You flinty-hearted rotter.

It is for the Sherlock Holmes Society to discover what actually drove Watson to lycanthropy, and whether a Mrs. M. Gidlake of Bayswater was, as he alleged, the witch who changed his shape at full moon. A man almost continuously stinko may easily have confused Mrs. Gidlake with some other lady.

Baker Street reflections

This is the season of exhibitions, and the most attractive are by no means confined to the South Bank of the Thames. It was a happy inspiration that guided the pens of those distinguished correspondents who first mooted, in the pages of *The Times*, the idea of a Sherlock Holmes Exhibition, and the local authority has risen magnificently to the occasion. Romance takes root in unexpected places; bedded in the native soil of the Metropolitan Borough of St. Marylebone, sheltered under the roof of the Abbey-National Building Society, a new plant has flowered, fair and fragrant amid the rank surrounding crop of byelaws and mortgage-deeds. Loving care and nature have brought to fruition a blossoming replica of the living-room at 221B, Baker Street, surrounded by lesser blooms of the most delightful varieties.

Here the physical eye can enjoy the Victorian interior pictured in the mind's eye of generations of admirers — the room where the Master lived and worked. Here is the famous dressing-gown, side by side with Dr. Watson's stethoscope, hanging on the inside of the door; there are the retorts used in Holmes's chemical experiments, and a hundred other objects vividly recalling the fascinating pages of Arthur Conan Doyle. There are "the diagrams, the violin-case and the pipe-rack . . . and a wax-coloured model of my friend, so admirably done that it was a perfect facisimile" (*The Empty House*). Nor are the great man's foibles concealed — vide *The Musgrave Ritual* — "his cigars in the coal-scuttle, his tobacco in the toe-end of a Persian slipper, and his unanswered correspondence transfixed by a jack-knife into the very centre of the wooden mantelpiece." (It is evident that his filing system, as well as his social habits, left much to be desired). There, too, is the permanent record of the occasion when "he would sit in an armchair, with his hair-trigger and a hundred Boxer cartridges, and proceed to adorn the opposite wall with a patriotic V.R. done in bullet-pocks" (*Ibid*).

In the past half-century Holmes has had innumerable imitators, but never an equal. "The science of deduction," as expounded in *A Study in Scarlet* and *The Sign of Four*, has proved too austere for this *dilettante* age. The so-called "detective-story" has either degenerated into the mere "thriller", packed with incidents of violence, and with few pretensions to literary style, or it has developed out of all recognition, into a psychological novel, usually of excessive complexity, and unsatisfactory in its *denouement*.

For the ordinary lawyer, who fortunately spends little of his professional life in close contact with violent crime, the fascination of Sherlock Holmes lies in the intellectual mastery of his deductive methods. Not for him the fanciful weaving of ingenious theories, miscalled "intuition," nor the blind acceptance of circumstantial evidence untested by the searching light of cross-examination. " 'The net is drawn pretty close round Fitzroy Simpson,' " says Inspector Gregory in *Silver Blaze*, " 'and I believe myself that he is our man' Holmes shook his head. 'A clever Counsel would tear it all to rags,' said he."

But the prime defect of the present-day "detective-story" is the cheap and easy way out of an *impasse* by means of a reconstruction of the crime, "third degree" methods and the convenient collapse and confession of the accused. Few crime-story writers appear to be acquainted with the strict rule of law that "the prosecution must prove affirmatively, to the satisfaction of the judge who tries the case that the admissions or confessions were not induced (*a*) by any promise of favour or advantage, (*b*) by the use of fear or threats or pressure, by a person in authority" (2 East, P.C. 657). Of the two classic instances quoted by Kenny (*Outlines of Criminal Law*, 15th edn., p. 470), "Tell, and you shall have some gin" speaks for itself, though the propriety of excluding a confession, made on the faith of this representation, has been doubted. As to the second, "If you will tell where the property is, you shall see your wife," (*R. v. Lloyd* (1834), 6 C. & P. 393), the learned author tactfully leaves the reader to infer for himself, according to taste, whether it was argued that these words fell under category *(a)* or *(b)* in the quotation from East, *supra.*

Aside from such elementary matters, Holmes knew well how to deal with that bugbear of the practising lawyer — the cunning client who thinks it clever to keep his adviser in the dark. " 'I cannot possibly advise you' " he tells Blessington, in *The Resident Patient*, " 'if you try to deceive me.' 'But I have told you everything.' Holmes turned on his heel with a gesture of disgust. 'Good-night, Dr. Trevelyan,' said he. 'And no advice for me?' cried Blessington, in a breaking voice. 'My advice to you, sir, is to speak the truth!' "

A large proportion of cases are won or lost before ever they come before the Court; painstaking preparation and careful analysis are of greater importance than brilliant advocacy. This is a truism by no means limited to criminal matters, and the Council of Legal Education and the Law Society might do well to consider the inclusion of the cases of Sherlock Holmes, in their *curriculum* of legal studies. Practitioners too, should be encouraged to give practical demonstrations of the method in training pupils in chambers and articled clerks.

CHAPLIN MEETS HOLMES

It is perhaps not widely known that in his early years Charlie Chaplin made a number of "straight" stage appearances both in London and the provinces. It is extremely difficult, however, to establish the exact chronology of these appearances, but a number of important dates are known.

Records show that he played in *Giddy Ostend* at the London Hippodrome on January 15, 1900. He would then have been ten years old. The play, of the "East Lynne" school, reflected both Charlie's actual life and his dream life. A street-waif to the last act, he then reunited his scattered family and won a fortune.

Young Chaplin received fine notices for his performance. He became quite a cocky young actor, enjoyed the life, dressed nattily, and sported a cane. This temporary prosperity enabled him to place his mother in a convalescent home, but despite the best of care she was never to regain her sanity.

Chaplin's income remained constant for three years, while he toured in *Sherlock Holmes* with H. A. Saintsbury in the lead and Chaplin himself as Billy, the office boy. Then, when William Gillette, the original American star of *Sherlock Holmes* came to London to star in the play, Chaplin was hired to resume the role of Billy.

The play opened late in 1905 at the Duke of York's Theatre, and in the company was a number of stage celebrities. Supporting Gillette in the play was the beautiful Marie Doro, later to star in American movies. She was one of Charlie's first crushes and he worshipped her from afar, afraid to approach her.

King Edward saw the performance one evening with Queen Alexandra and the King of Greece. The actors were ordered not to look at the royal box, but Charlie could not resist the temptation. There was an awful stillness in the audience until a chuckle from King Edward broke the silence. Chaplin was scolded, but exultant that he had amused royalty.

A success in his role, he expected to be invited back to America with

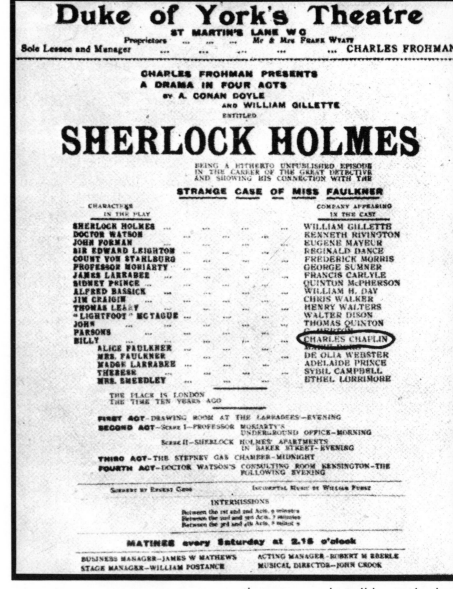

Charlie Chaplin — and the playbill that announced his appearance in "The Strange Case of Miss Faulker" (1905).

the company, but all he received from Gillette was a pat on the shoulder. A lean period followed during his "awkward age." He found work in a glass factory, but this lasted only one day. He burned his hand and could not stand the extreme heat. So back to the stage he went, getting occasional bookings in burlesque. One was with The Ten Looneys; and as a single turn he was billed as Sam Cohen, the Jewish Comedian, however, success as a comic, lay just around the corner . . .

Punch November 21 1951

Double Bluff

Said Watson to Holmes "Is it wise –
Such false whiskers when hunting for spies?"
Said the sleuth, "I'm afraid
You're as dense as Lestrade:
I'm disguised as myself in disguise."

Daily Express Thursday May 24 1951

HOLMES BEATS THE YARD

A burglar's kit (1890 variety) which includes skeleton keys and a full range of jemmies has been lent by an anonymous Londoner to the Sherlock Holmes exhibition at 221B Baker Street, Marylebone.

Scotland Yard disapproves. The Yard lent handcuffs, firearms, and bullets that had been used by murderers, but told the organisers:

"An 1890 burglar's kit could be used in 1951. We are not willing to risk someone snatching it."

The People January 6 1952

HANNEN SWAFFER SAYS . .
Spreading "Culture"

Well, if the Festival of Britain did nothing else for culture, it at least boosted detective fiction.

The Borough of St. Marylebone, indeed, claims that its Sherlock Holmes Exhibition in Baker Street, was the only Festival venture that paid its way.

Among the visitors was one elderly woman who said to another, "I wonder where Sherlock Holmes was buried."

"Don't be silly," was the reply. "Holmes was only a fictitious character."

"Oh, I see," said her friend, "like William Shakespeare."

Look April 22 1952

JOHN LARDNER'S NEW YORK
Another Rewrite

Mickey Spillane, statistics show, is one of the hottest numbers in modern literature. In hardback and paperback editions, his detective stories have sold something like 11 million copies. Make that 11 million and one, because I recently bought an early Spillane called "The Big Kill", in self-defence against Berle in Richmond and quarter radios in South Carolina. This Spillane lives in Newburgh, N.Y., a small piece from the great city. His private eye hero, Mike Hammer, is an ever-guzzling, ever-loving, ever-shooting, ever-sapping son-of-a-gun—like most shamuses in books, only more so. Spillane, himself, on the other hand, so I'm told, has just joined the religious sect called Jehovah's Witnesses. Maybe Hammer's bad habits are getting on his nerves.

Whether Hammer is a sadist, a heel, and a rake, or not, I want to state for the record that he comes straight out of Sherlock Holmes, the champion gumshoe of sixty years ago. All storybook private eyes do. Dashiell Hammett gets a lot of credit, and rightly, for his influence on the style of modern detective fiction, but I have been mixing Conan Doyle with Spillane in my reading lately, and I'm surer than ever that whatever these modern dicks do, Holmes did first and better.

Spillane's man, Hammer ("I kill mad dogs"), wants to rid the city of evil all by himself. So he empties his .45 into the soft intestines of bad men. But Holmes, in his time, knocked off at least two hoodlums personally. He bumped the great Professor Moriarty by the use of baritsu (Japanese wrestling). And he killed another mad dog by throwing a deadly snake (a swamp adder) right back at him.

Hammer insults cops. He spits on the district attorney's floor. But Holmes was the original baiter of the official police. He laughed in the teeth of Scotland Yard, and that's been the style ever since.

Hammer pours liquor down his gullet. But Holmes topped him by hitting the main line (injecting himself) with cocaine. And he smoked tobacco that drove Dr. Watson to cover.

Dames? Well, Hammer talks a big romance, while Holmes was cool to tomatoes, or women as they called them then. But, who was it who posed as a plumber and promised to marry a blackmailer's housemaid, in order to get the goods on her boss? No one but the greatest shamus of them all, S. Holmes. The rest are imitations.

Reveille June 8 1952

When a Sherlock Holmes exhibition opens in New York in July there will be dust on the floor. The dust has been collected in Baker Street, London where Holmes is said to have lived, and shipped to New York.

John O'London's Weekly October 10 1952

A SHERLOCKIAN COINCIDENCE!

We have learned that the Undergraduates at Pembroke College, Cambridge this term include a Mr. Sherlock and a Mr. Holmes and that they have been allotted rooms on the same staircase. The Master S. C. Roberts, happens to be President of the Sherlock Holmes Society of London, and was unaware of this fact until pointed out to him. He has since hinted darkly that the arrangement "might well be the work of Professor Moriarty."

The Spectator June 5 1953

HOLMES, SWEET HOLMES

I remember seeing William Gillette as Sherlock Holmes at the Lyceum Theatre just fifty years ago and I feel sure one is correct in saying that "elementary, my dear Watson" was a line in the play. Gillette spoke in an eerie, sinister drawl, rather high-pitched, and, with his head thrown back and eyes half-closed, gave the impression that he was thinking of anything but the problem on hand. Only at the tense moments with Moriarty did he snap into life and become peremptory and incisive. There was at the same period a skit on Gillette as Holmes running at Terry's Theatre in the Strand, called Picklock Holes, and the phrase was used in that as well.

Charlie Chaplin played the page boy in the Lyceum "Holmes" and he used to dash on the stage with his uniform in tatters indicative of his struggle with Moriarty's men who had tried, off stage, to stop him reaching Holmes. No doubt Mr. Chaplin would be as good an authority as any on the use of the line on the stage.

AUBREY VINCENT

SHERLOCK'S SHAG

The point is — did Sherlock Holmes smoke a particularly foul tobacco or was his shag merely a fine-cut Virginia leaf? After all, he was something of a connoisseur of wine. Would he, then, ruin his palate with rank tobacco?

What does it matter, you say. Not to ordinary people perhaps. But it does to the members of the Sherlock Holmes Society of London. At their last meeting in Baker Street, Colonel Sherbrooke-Walker read a most instructive paper on Holmes's and Watson's taste in tobacco. And, as always at the meetings a lively discussion followed. Poor old Watson, it was agreed, had little taste in anything; but the Master — he knew a good cigar and, if you remember, wrote a monograph on cigar ash. Surely the toe of that famous Persian slipper held a decent tobacco? Personally, I like to think it did.

The Daily Telegraph May 26 1952

HOLMES SHOW IN NEW YORK
Curator Seeks A "Red Leech"

One of the most careworn men in New York to-day was Mr. C. T. Thorne, 36, curator of the Sherlock Holmes exhibition. It will shortly be seen by New Yorkers.

The exhibition was brought over here after its successful London run last year by Mr. Adrian Conan Doyle, youngest son of Holmes's creator. It is at present lodged in a New York warehouse.

When I called on Mr. Thorne at his hotel to-day his air was troubled and reflective. "My problem is that I have to find a live snake — an easy task, but the complications that go with it are little short of frightful," he said.

Mr. Thorne, who needs a snake to illustrate "The Speckled Band" story continued: "I approached the hotel management here and asked them: 'Am I allowed to keep pets in my bed-room?' They replied: 'No dogs or cats are allowed.' "

No snakes allowed

"When I told them that I did not want to keep a dog or a cat, but a snake, they nearly had a fit. They said that if the word got round it would clear the hotel."

He added with a smile: "I wonder what they would think if they knew I had a remarkable worm unknown to science already in my bed-room, to say nothing of a couple of leeches."

He said leeches were another of his problems. "Dr. Watson refers to the 'repulsive story of the red leech' and 'death of Crosby the Banker' " he explained. "There is no direct evidence how Crosby died but the theory is that a leech may have got into his nostrils or windpipe and choked him as it fed on his blood."

"Now there are 64 varieties of medicinal leeches alone, but no leech of any kind has been found which is completely red. I may eventually have to try cross-breeding leeches like geraniums in an attempt to get the right colour."

Aluminium doubt

He was also perplexed by Watson's reference to "the singular case of the aluminium crutch." He found that Holmes was most likely engaged on that case between 1877 and 1880. The question was whether aluminium crutches existed at that time.

"The nearest thing I have got to proving it is a treatise written by de Ville, the French aluminium pioneer, in 1859. It deals with the use of aluminium in surgical equipment."

Mr. Thorpe has been a reference librarian of St. Marylebone Borough Council for 18 years. He was given a year's leave by the Council to accompany the Holmes exhibition.

"My job made me a stickler for authenticity," he said. "Until I am satisfied a thing has a reasonable chance of being genuine I would not dream of putting it in the exhibition."

The Times July 17 1952

THE ULTIMA THULE OF ROMANCE

I have been through one of the most thrilling experiences of my life, and I am rushing to write to you about it while the magic of it is still fresh in my mind. When we first read of the possibility that the Sherlock Holmes exhibition might come to America, we thought it was too good to be true, but there must be some patron saint of Sherlockians who heard our prayers, for our dream has been realized beyond all our expectations.

I have seen at first hand the wonderful collections of *memorablia* of Sir Arthur Conan Doyle and Sherlock Holmes; I have seen the Norwood notebook, specimens of *Cyanea Capillata*, Russell's Viper, the red leech of repulsive fame, and the remarkable worm, still unknown to science. I have stood on the platform outside the marvellous reconstruction of 221b and fallen under the spell of that never-never land which has captivated me since my earliest years.

I know every detail of that fairyland as intimately as I know every nook and corner of my own home — even more so, as I never remember where I have put my eyeglasses, but I can tell you to a square inch the location of the harpoon that killed Black Peter, the Persian slipper with the shag tobacco, the picklocks in the butterdish, Holmes's commonplace books and Beecher's unframed portrait.

There is a wonderous aura about that poem that dispels any last doubt the sceptic may have as to the reality of Sherlock Holmes and Dr. Watson. The glow of the lamps, the clop-clop of the hansom heard in the sound track, the tick-tock of the mantel clock which miraculously keeps the same time hour after hour — all these things heighten the ineluctable illusion of reality. It is truly the Ultima Thule of romance.

NATHAN L. BENGIS
Keeper of the Crown,
The Musgrave Ritualists,
West 188 Street,
New York.

Right: A drawing by Wyndham Robinson of "The Legendary Figure" in which Holmes' reviews some of his cases. The "Strand Magazine", 1948.

Wyndham Robinson

The mystery of Baskerville

Thousands of devoted admirers of Sherlock Holmes, the Baker-street detective to whom all things were elementary, will be surprised this morning by a new mystery — a real life one — which sprang up last night.

It is a mystery which may well become as legendary as the bitter, long-running Bacon-Shakespeare controversy.

For, after more than 50 years, the authorship of one of the best-known Holmes stories, "The Hound of the Baskervilles," is being disputed.

And disputed by no less an authority than the man the story is named after, Harry Baskerville.

Last night I drove to a small, narrow-streeted village in the silent shadow of Dartmoor to talk to wispy, white-haired Baskerville, who claims that a brilliant young journalist, who was soon to die in mysterious circumstances, helped Doyle write the great thriller.

Pink-faced and younger-looking than his 88 years, Baskerville told me in a firm, fine Devonshire voice:—

"Doyle didn't write the story himself. A lot of the story was written by Fletcher Robinson. But he never got the credit he deserved.

"They wrote it together at Park Hill, over at Ipplepen. I know, because I was there."

Baskerville, who was a coachman to Robinson's father, told me that long before Doyle arrived at Park Hill, in Devon, Fletcher Robinson had confided:—

"Harry, I'm going to write a story about the moor and I would like to use your name."

Clutching a fading, yellow-leafed, brown-paper-backed first edition of the book — with the handwritten inscription: "To Harry Baskerville from B. Fletcher Robinson. With apologies for using the name" — Baskerville went on:

"Shortly after his return from the Boer War, Bertie (Robinson) told me to meet Mr. Doyle at the station. He said they were going to work on the story he had told me about.

"Mr. Doyle stayed for eight days and nights. I had to drive him and Bertie about the moors. And I used to watch them in the billiards room in the old house, sometimes they stayed long into the night, writing and talking together.

"Then Mr. Doyle left and Bertie said to me:

'Well, Harry, we've finished that book I was telling you about. The one we're going to name after you.' "

But last night, Baskerville's story was angrily denied by Sir Arthur Conan Doyle's son Adrian.

When I phoned him in Geneva, Switzerland, where he now lives, he said:—

"Fletcher Robinson wrote not one word of the story. He refused my father's offer to collaborate and retired at an early stage of the project.

"Furthermore, my father never stayed with Robinson. He stayed at the Duchy Hotel, Princetown. He accepted Robinson's offer of a coach and went riding with him on the moors simply to get the atmosphere of the place.

"In fact, I have letters from Robinson proving this. It was Robinson who told my father about a West Country legend, but that was just about the extent of his contribution."

Indeed, in a short preface to the book, author Doyle wrote: "My dear Robinson, it was to your account of a West Country legend that this tale owes its inception. For this and for your help in the details, all thanks." But was this enough? Baskerville is convinced Robinson played a larger part.

"There was never such a legend. It was a story Bertie invented and helped to write. I don't know why he didn't get more credit. It didn't seem to worry him, though," he said.

Soon after the publication of the book mystery-man Robinson — described by a 1907 newspaper cutting as the author of many "thrilling detective stories" — started a fateful investigation into an Egyptian mummy's curse.

Before he could complete his research he died. He was 35.

When Doyle heard of his death he said: "I warned him against concerning himself with the mummy. I told him he was tempting fate by pursuing his inquiries, but he was fascinated and would not desist. Then he was overtaken with illness.

"He was the last man in the world to want to die — strong, vigorous, and in excellent physical condition — but he died.

"The immediate cause of death was typhoid fever, but that is the way in which the 'elementals' guarding the mummy might act."

With the sudden, sad death of Robinson the possibility of his co-authorship was forgotten — except by one man, Baskerville.

Could he have contributed more than the world has realised?

A Holmes expert told me: "This could explain the big mystery of why Holmes appears so infrequently in the Hound.

"We know that when Doyle wrote the story he had already killed off Holmes — whom he disliked and regarded as a pot-boiler in 'The Final Problem.'

"If this information is correct, it is just possible that Doyle, faced with a public outcry for killing his hero, had to quickly produce another Holmes story.

"He may have agreed with Fletcher Robinson to adapt an existing Robinson story but found it impossible to make Holmes the central figure."
And in London last night the mystery deepened. A member of the Sherlock Holmes Society told me:—

"This sounds like the story James Montgomery was working on. He was a rich American, a member of the Baker-street Irregulars (the American Sherlock Holmes Society) and he came to Britain about three years ago to interview Baskerville.

"He hinted at his discoveries but refused to say very much because he was planning to publish a monograph.

"He was very excited and talked about startling discoveries. But he returned to America and within three weeks he was dead. The monograph was never published and his notes were never found."

It is a curious story. A mystery worthy of the brain of Baker Street himself. But I'm afraid he would discover little that is elementary.

Left: Harry Baskerville. This page: The poster for the latest film of "The Hound of the Baskervilles" and three frames from the strip cartoon of the story by Edith Meiser and Frank Giacoia 1954-5.

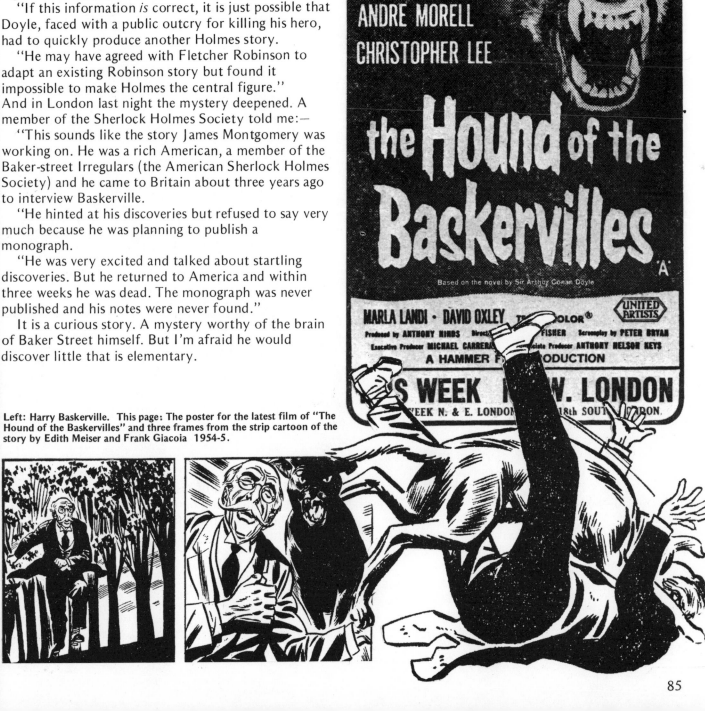

SADLER'S WELLS THEATRE BALLET "THE GREAT DETECTIVE"

The career of Mr. Sherlock Holmes, which takes a justly prominent place in the annals of Victorian history, has not before provided the inspiration for ballet, we think. Margaret Dale and Richard Arnell, who, together with Brian Robb, have made the new ballet at Sadler's Wells, bring to the stage some hitherto unrecorded pages from the memoirs of his Boswell, Dr. Watson; they do not allude by name to their characters, and that understandably, for the events here shown are more bizarre than Mr. Holmes's most fervent admirers will credit.

We see the Detective and his friend engaged in saving an innocent man from wrongful arrest; we see the infamous Professor (let him not be named) at his astonishing machinations, and we see the Detective as he tames a dangerous gorilla and — in silhouette — grapples with his enemy. The choregraphic invention and the material of some episodes are droll, but one is glad to find the Detective presented in a properly heroic light, alert, precise and fearless; his pipe and his violin are introduced, but not the hypodermic syringe with which malicious gossip (even passed on by his biographer) has sometimes connected him — it was a laudable, though surely inevitable, omission.

Miss Dale's own humorous dancing (as we have admired it in *Facade* and *Bonne-Bouche*) is reflected in the athletic *grotesquerie* of her choreography, and some of her ideas are cleverly comical. Perhaps Mr. Robb, who has designed the gay scenery and costumes, must claim part of the credit for the ingeniously contrived marionettes tyrannized by the Professor. Arnell's music suits the world here evoked, in its staid yet full-blooded and also kindly gaiety. Mr. Stanley Holden danced with *elan*, but made Dr. Watson more of the Edwardian masher than his writings suggest. Mr. Kenneth Macmillan zealously portrayed the Detective, and doubled the role of the Professor, with virtuosity in the final scene. But this dual role is not only an artist's fiction; it is a dangerous gloss on history. We cannot allow posterity to infer that our beloved Mr. Holmes and the vile Moriarty are one and the same person. Has Dr. Watson been duping his readers? Mr. Holmes must be persuaded, in his well earned retirement, to take pen and refute the damaging suggestion.

MY DEAR WATSON! BY RICHARD BUCKLE

A Sherlock Holmes ballet? Well, one can imagine a severely stylised and classical work to a Mozart divertimento. The first movement an appeal for help in Baker-street; the *andante* a train journey from Paddington into the autumnal West Country; the theme and variations a propounding of possible solutions to the crime; the finale a triumph of the master mind, celebrated — with just a hint of "Character" colouring — by the rural police. Or there is the romantic Betjeman approach — for we must remember that the Holmes stories are read to-day for the nostalgic picture they evoke of gas-lit, fog-bound London in the nineties, of hansoms bowling between marmoreal clubs in Pall Mall and creeper-covered villas in Camberwell, where retired irascible merchants are tended by gong-sounding maids. Miss Margaret Dale, who, television apart, was making her cheoreographic *debut* at Sadler's Wells on Wednesday, had neither of these ideas; in fact I find it hard to see what her idea was or why she picked on Holmes at all. She clearly meant to make a screamingly funny ballet — a dangerous ambition, for ballet rarely succeeds in being funny for more than a few seconds at a time.

The Great Detective is a phantasmagoria of corpses, murderers, policemen, distressed ladies, a gorilla, human puppets from some quite different mythology, and two unaccountably Regency sailors. Holmes in deerstalker and Inverness cape was clearly recognisable, threading his way through no particular mystery, but Moriarty, also played by Kenneth Macmillan, looked thirty years too young; and my *dear*! — Watson! Stanley Holden's conception (or his choreographer's) of the excellent Doctor as a swaggering little elderly *beau* was thoroughly inappropriate and all to reminiscent of Pantalon in *Carnaval.* Alas! The ballet is just a silly muddle; and as for knowing if Miss Dale has gifts for choreography or not, we are back where we were before. Richard Arnell is always an interesting composer, and what little of his music I could take in at first hearing seemed too grown-up for so innocent an occasiori. The designs of Brian Robb, showing various influences from Picasso to Dufy, but never a trace of the good old "Strand Magazine," added the last straw of incongruity to this misadventure of Sherlock Holmes.

Above and previous pages: Two photographs from the Sadler's Wells Ballet "The Great Detective" with Kenneth Macmillan and Stanley Holden as Holmes and Watson respectively (1953).

By permission of the
Trustees of the Estate
of Sir Arthur
Conan Doyle

What did Dr. Watson say to Holmes?

I'll have a Mann's Brown!

MANN'S BROWN

makes everyone friends

Mann's Brown is Britain's best Brown Ale

1953

The Baker Street Irregulars of New York

On a foggy and drizzling evening in January, 1950, at a club in New York City, 50 men drank a standing toast. It was in regret and homage to their own boyhoods; it was occasioned by the soon approaching demise of the "Strand Magazine." Some 30 of the convives were members of the Baker Street Irregulars, a club whose membership is limited to 60 — the number of the Sherlock Holmes stories. The others were delegates from "scionist" societies, viz., satellite chapters from other faubourgs of cities, of which there are about 30.

Surely it is a unique tribute to an author whose name, officially, is never mentioned. The traditional *mystique* is that Holmes and Watson are so much more real than their creator that except by privilege from the Chair (known as The Gasogene) the Agent is never mentioned by name.

The fundamental doctrine of the B.S.I., when they set aside for an evening the irrelevant trivialities of their own lives, is that the Holmes-Watson saga (officially denominated by Mr. Elmer Davis "THE SACRED WRITINGS") is more actual, and more timely, than anything that happens to ourselves or happened to its mortal mouthpiece. The greatest art is the annihilation of art.

I once went to Somerset House, or whatever it's called, to "search" the will of Sir Arthur Conan Doyle. I couldn't help wondering whether in his final testimony he had made any mention of his humble passports to immortaility. I paid my shilling (just as Holmes used to at "Doctors' Commons") and read the document, in his own clear masculine hand — so like the map of the Priory School neighbourhood. Not a word about the incubus Holmes . . . and yet Holmes, even in profile and robe and headgear, is pretty nearly the Dante of our modern inferno.

With profound insight the B.S.I. have adopted as their colours the three shades of Holmes's dressing gown. It faded as all mortal energies do; from royal purple to blemished blue; from heliotroped blue to mouse. Mouse, by the way, was the colour of the settees in Simpson's famous Chess Divan, as reported in R.L.S.'s "New Arabian Nights," from which A.C.D. unconsciously borrowed so much.

So the B.S.I. published for three years a quarterly journal (whose motto was: "When was so much written by so many for so few?"), but if you can get from your bookseller (Argus Bookshop, Mohegan Lake, N.Y.) those three volumes you will have the best winter evening reading of a lifetime. Myself, I would rather have them than a first Bristol Cream of Wordsworth and Coleridge's "Lyrical Ballads."

Wordsworth and S.T.C. were also greatly anxious about affairs in 1798. But now we need to know, as Holmes asked Watson. "What do you know of the black Formosa corruption?" How I would have loved to ask Madame Generalissima Chiang that question, just before she took off by plane lately — she is obviously the Irene Adler of South-East Asia.

Or when Holmes spent the great hiatus (1891-94) in Tibet, wasn't he making arrangements 60 years ahead for what's getting ready now? Or the reptilian Moriarty oscillating his cobra brow over the dynamics of an asteroid, was doubtless precursing uranium and hydrogen bombs, all fission spent. What could the great untold story of the Politician, the Lighthouse, and the Trained Cormorant have suggested but the career of Sir Stafford Cripps?

These are the hints the B.S.I. follow through. Why did passengers on the G.W.R. *have* to take lunch at Swindon? Exactly how (and with what type scalpel) do you nick the tendons of a horse? What was the precise layout of the rooms in Baker Street? Was Sherlock illiterate, I mean could he read? Why did Watson always have to read aloud to him all letters and telegrams? Why did Holmes never eat fish but always game, beef, and boiled eggs; Why did he never drink tea? Why was he such a poor marksman? These are the parleipses or paralipomena to which we devote the most innocent diversion of our lives.

Myself I do not wholly agree with the tradition that A.C.D. should never be formally mentioned. I loved him long before his heirs and assigns and agents were born, and I find in his writings the most delicious asymptotes to the Holmes-Watson codex. As I have often said, how ridiculous he was only Knighted — he should have been Sainted.

My Christmas carol of last year was this:

What opiate can best abate Anxiety and toil?

Not aspirins, nor treble gins, Nor love, nor mineral oil —

My only drug is a good long slug Of Tincture of Conan Doyle.

Now *there's* a tobacco you could smoke all day without burning your tongue.

Amazing, Holmes!

Elementary, my dear Watson—it's

Grand Cut

Never burns the tongue of old or young   2 oz 8/2

ISSUED BY GODFREY PHILLIPS LIMITED

1954

THE SHERLOCK HOLMES SPECIAL

Sherlock Holmes will ride from No. 4 platform at London's Baker Street station tomorrow at 3 p.m.

Before the war there were about twenty electric locos running from Baker Street. One of them was called Sherlock Holmes, but the plates were removed. I understand it was the idea of Mr. Roberts, the 66-year-old Master of Pembroke College, Cambridge, trustee of Shakespeare's birthplace and Johnsonian scholar, that the Sherlock Holmes Society of London should put them back.

"S.C.," as Mr. Roberts is known to Cambridge men, will be present, with about 50 members of the society, including the Marquess of Donegall, possessor of the world's best collection of Holmes first editions.

No rules on dress have been issued with the invitations, but some deerstalkers and even an Inverness cape may be on view.

Above: Sherlock Holmes and Dr. Watson arrive by train in "The Adventure of the Dancing Man" (1903). The invitation ticket was issued some 50 years later when London Transport inaugurated their 'Sherlock Holmes' underground train with a special ceremony. The noted Sherlockian, Dr. S.C. Roberts, officiated at the gathering.

The Chairman and Members of
THE LONDON TRANSPORT EXECUTIVE
request the pleasure of the company of

Mr. Weston

at

BAKER STREET STATION
(Platform No. 3)

on Monday, 5th October, 1953, at 3.0 p.m.

FOR THE CEREMONY OF NAMING ONE OF THE LONDON TRANSPORT ELECTRIC LOCOMOTIVES "SHERLOCK HOLMES"

and for the inaugural trip departing from Baker Street at 3.20 p.m.

The Sunday Times February 5
1950

THE IRREGULARS AND SOME IMPONDERABLES

Mr. Christopher Morley's charming article cannot fail to stir those like myself whose spiritual home has always been 221B, Baker Street, I found especially engaging the suggestion that some of the 'untold' Holmes-Watson stories glance at the shape of things to come, and in particular that the story of the "Trained Cormorant" foreshadowed the career of Sir Stafford Cripps. Having lifted a corner of this curtain I hope Mr. Morley will go on and tell us what politician of what party is prefigured in some of the other 'untold' stories: e.g. the "Adventure of the Tired Captain" and the "Repulsive affair of the red leech."

Mr. Morley asks: "Was Holmes illiterate? I mean, could he read?": and points out how often Holmes delegates the reading of notes and letters to Watson. Personally I think this was pure affectation. He needed no help from Watson in deciphering the letter written in alternative words by the Cunninghams in the "Reigate Squires." As to books, although Watson describes his friend's knowledge of literature in disparaging terms, Holmes had read (and Watson had not) Winwood Reade's "Martyrdom of Man."

Mr. Morley rightly stresses Holme's addiction to game (he is fantastically voracious of woodcock) and eggs. But "boiled" eggs? In those spacious days Mrs. Hudson generally combined her eggs with ham, and this almost necessarily implies an absence of shell.

And was Holmes a "poor marksman"? He emptied five barrels of his revolver "into" the flanks of the Hound of the Baskervilles and therefore presumably hit it. Mr. Morely may say that having regard to the size of the Hound it would be as difficult to miss him as a haystack at point-blank range. But the same cannot be said of the "patriotic V.R." traced with the punctures of revolver bullets, with which Holmes decorated the walls of his Baker Street rooms.

The oldest puzzle of all (raised as far back as 1910 by Monsignor Knox, "the father of English Watsonology") was why an Afgan bullet which hit Watson in the shoulder caused him, for the rest of his life, to limp. Can the "Baker Street Irregulars" supply the answer? And have they any views as to whether Watson (a) was a dipsomaniac, (b) married twice, (c) married three times?

The evidence for the first two of these propositions is impressive; but I entertain some doubts about the third.

LORD JUSTICE ASQUITH
Royal Courts of Justice..

The Sunday Times February 12
1950

WAS WATSON A WOMAN?

Lord Justice Asquith revives an old puzzle concerning Dr. Watson — was he married twice, or three times? Students of the Sacred Writings may recall that this question was debated in part by the "Baker Street Irregulars" themselves, on a memorable occasion when one of their members put to these most reverent of all Sherlock Holmes's disciples the most irreverent proposition in their records.

In New York, on January 31, 1941 — "a date that lives in infamy for all the faithful" — Mr. Rex Stout, bearded creator of Nero Wolfe, refused to join the commemorative toast, "The Second Mrs. Watson." It was a matter of conscience, Stout said. He could not bring himself to connive at the perpetration of a hoax. Not only was there never a second Mrs. Watson; there was not even a first Mrs. Watson. Furthermore, there was no Doctor Watson. "She" was a woman!

After producing a mass of heretical "evidence," Stout, "by methods that Holmes himself might have used," proceeded to look into the immortal tales for a record of the "woman" Watson's full name. He took all 60 tales set them down in chronological order, numbered them from 1 to 60. Then, by an ingenious process of elimination, he got them down to

Illustrious Client,
Red-Headed League,
Engineer's Thumb
Norwood Builder
Empty House,

Wisteria Lodge,
Abbey Grange,
Twisted Lip,
Study in Scarlet,
Orange Pips,
Noble Bachelor.

"And, acrostically simple, the initial letters read down, the carefully hidden secret is ours," said Stout. "Her name was Irene Watson."

Stout ended by telling the apoplectic "Irregulars" he was collecting material for a fuller treatment of the subject . . . "It will fill two volumes, the second of which will consist of certain speculations regarding various concrete results of that long-continued and — I fear, alas — none-too-happy union (between Holmes and this "woman"). For instance, what of the parentage of Lord Peter Wimsey, who was born, I believe, around the turn of the century — about the time of the publication of 'The Adventure of the Second Stain'? That will bear looking into."

Can one wonder that (to quote Mr. Howard Haycraft) even after the passage of years, Mr. Stout attends the annual festivities of the august and nominally peace-loving "Irregulars" only when accompanied by a personal bodyguard?

A.R. McELWAIN, Fleet Street, E.C.4.

Daily Express June 2 1959

BROKEN BIG TOE
Killed a man

A blood clot caused by a broken big toe killed Arthur Ernest Sherlock Holmes aged 51 of Bedminster, Bristol it was said at a Bristol inquest yesterday. Verdict: an accident

The Tatler August 12 1953

WATSON TYRANISED
BY D.B. WYNDHAM LEWIS

"What the devil do you mean," snarls a truculent Sherlock Holmes fan inflamed by our expose of a fascinating new Baker Street problem in this page by saying that 'Watson, for once, was sober'?" We mean, chum, that John H. Watson, M.D., late Indian Army, was, for once, not under the influence of alcohol.

Apart from the question of hypocrisy, it seems to us a great disservice to Doc Watson to maintain that ridiculous conspiracy of silence over his only failing. Those increasing snifters which nerved him to endure Holmes's tyranny might not have undermined a less amiable character; and in fact on learning that Professor Moriarty has successfully tossed Holmes off the Reichenbach, Watson took a fresh grip on life, joined the Band of Hope, forgot his old Afghan wound, and was seen dancing round a cup of tea in his surgery ("I'm youth, I'm joy, I'm a little bird that has broken out of the egg!") On Holmes's dismaying reappearance Watson's wine-merchant could start rubbing his hands again. The removal of Watson's name from the Medical Register was henceforth only a matter of time.

Possibly the British Medical Association boys were too harsh? Watson was not often in his consulting-room during the long Holmes regime and when there he was far too cockeyed for proper diagnosis or prescription. By this means hundreds of human lives must have been saved. BMA, you're out.

The People July 12 1953

HANNEN SWAFFER SAYS . . .
Was Sherlock A Fool?

Was Sherlock Holmes merely an "opinionated busybody" — behind the times? Or did Conan Doyle, his creator, transform crime investigation?

Christopher Pulling, the Yard's senior assistant secretary, declared that Sherlock Holmes, although he habitually sneered at the London police, used "dirty and nasty methods" that, if adopted by Scotland Yard would have foisted "guilt for a revolting statesman or Church dignitary!"

So, naturally, Doyle's two sons, Denis and Adrian, have risen in anger.

"The police systems of the modern world," they reply, "are founded on the new ideas in criminology, expressed by our father in his detective stories."

"Father invented the use of plaster of paris for preserving footprints," claim Doyle's sons, "the minute examination of dust on a man's clothes to discover his occupation or where he had been, and the precise differentiation among various tobacco ashes."

The only time I met J. Edgar Hoover, head of the F.B.I. — it was at a New York lunch — he began his speech by saying: "As a well-known London journalist is present, I will not say what I think of Scotland Yard."

Hannen Swaffer, the noted Fleet Street columnist, meets Sherlock Holmes
and asks — Did the Master Detective transform crime investigation?

AN OLD FRIEND'S BIRTHDAY

To-night the B.B.C. celebrates the hundredth birthday of Mr. Sherlock Holmes. Some successors of his, both imaginary and real, headed by Lord Peter Wimsey, will pay tribute to his genius. We can only wish that the shades of two of his mighty predecessors had been evoked to do him similar honour, Inspector Bucket and Sergeant Cuff. That would have been quite a party. Exactly how the date of his birth has been arrived at we do not yet know. The chronology of the Holmes stories has engaged some of the brightest intellects in this country. Their mental gymnastics have sometimes been so brilliant as to seem almost exhausting. That at least is the view of many a common man who yields to none in his adoration of the master. When all is said, most of us, devoted though we be, are intellectually no better than good, honest, plodding Watsons. There are about us unexpected possibilities of stupidity. In our humble, fundamentalist faith we take the sacred writings as we find them. We no more believe that, as hinted by perhaps the most sparkling of all the commentators, Mycroft Holmes was in league with Professor Moriarty than that Watson contracted a second marriage with Miss de Melville.

For such as us a simple clue or two will suffice. In His Last Bow Holmes, when in the guise of Altamont, is described as "a tall gaunt man of sixty." That adventure happened beyond question in 1914, on the eve of war, and so points to 1854 as the year of the birth. More complex and dubious evidence is derived from Holmes's career at Cambridge. MISS DOROTHY SAYERS, a great authority (though some respectfully think she went astray as to his college), believes that he was a third year man in 1874. That too suggests 1854, the year favoured by a scholar of vast erudition, MR. H. W. BELL; but it is fair to add that others have argued for 1853 or even 1852. However, as we have lately seen a mistake made as to an illustrious contemporary, SIR HERBERT TREE, perhaps a single year does not matter.

This celebration of a famous character's birthday is not unique, for when Mr. Pickwick's centenary came around some years ago a large company drank his health at dinner to the strains of "He's a jolly good fellow." But Mr. Pickwick's sitting-room on the first floor front in Goswell Street has never been reconstructed for his admirers, whereas during the Festival of Britain many worshippers made pilgrimage to the model of 221B Baker Street, exactly as it had been in Mrs. Hudson's day. We have no positive information where Mr. Holmes will keep his anniversary, but there seems no reason to doubt that he still lives surrounded by his faithful bees on the South Downs. "Nothing of interest in the paper, Watson?" We can fancy him saying, harking back, as old men will, and then lighting with pleasure on his own name. If any listeners feel disposed to raise their glasses to him to-night, they must not fear lest his cold and reserved nature should disdain their homage. Let them remember how, in the little affair of the six Napoleons, he bowed to his audience when they broke into spontaneous clapping. "Thank you," he said, "thank you," and turned away to hide his emotion.

TANFIELD'S DIARY

THE SHADOW OF MORIARTY STILL DARKENS BAKER STREET

It is possible that the heirs of the evil Professor Moriarty are behind this confusion which exists over the age of Sherlock Holmes? Someone, it seems, is producing all sorts of odd evidence on the date of the great detective's birth.

Last night the B.B.C. held a party to celebrate Holmes's 100th birthday, and in America the Baker-street Irregulars — who decided that Holmes was born in 1854 — also celebrated.

The Americans decided on January 6 because in the last story, "His Last Bow," set in early August 1914, Watson describes Holmes as a man of 60.

Britain's Sherlock Holmes Society have agreed to this date for the sake of uniformity — but only with "characteristic reservations," I was told yesterday.
But unknown "researchers" in many parts of the world have been producing conflicting evidence on Holmes's age. Keen amateur crimonologists want to know who has been sowing these seeds of confusion.

Our experts here point out that Holmes was disguised with a goatee beard in "His Last Bow" and "looked a man of 60," which did not necessarily mean he was 60.

Mr. James Holroyd, a member of the Council of the Sherlock Holmes Society, tells me that an American doctor has been busy making an elaborate chronology of the great detective's life and he makes the year of birth either 1858 or 1859. This month, I am told, a plaque is to be unveiled at St. Bartholomew's Hospital to commemorate the first meeting of Dr. Watson and Sherlock Holmes.

A Swiss caricature published in 1954 to celebrate Holmes' 100th Birthday.

AT THIS PLACE NEW YEARS DAY, 1881 WERE SPOKEN THESE DEATHLESS WORDS

"YOU HAVE BEEN IN AFGHANISTAN, I PERCEIVE."

BY

Mr. SHERLOCK HOLMES

IN GREETING TO

JOHN H. WATSON, M.D.

AT THEIR FIRST MEETING

THE BAKER STREET IRREGULARS — 1953
BY THE AMATEUR MENDICANTS AT THE CAUCUS CLUB.

Above: The 'Afghanistan' plaque errected in January 1954 by American enthusiasts to commemorate the first meeting of Holmes and Watson at St. Bartholomew's Hospital in London. Below: Mycroft Holmes, Sherlock's brother.

John O'London's Weekly March 19 1954

TEA-TIME TALES

I wonder if any other "old girls" who were at the Convent at Roehampton as far back as 1902 remember a nun telling some of the Sherlock Holmes stories during the tea break?

Tea consisted of bread-and-jam and cold water, but the thrilling way in which she told us the adventure of "The Engineer's Thumb" compensated one listener at least for the absence of real tea!

HELEN EASTWOOD,
St. Agnes, Cornwall

John O'London's March 26 1954

"THE PARADOL CHAMBER"

I have seen that in 'John O'London's Column' he is speculating on the meaning of the word Paradol in Sherlock Holmes' mention of "The Adventure of the Paradol Chamber". Paradol is a pain-killing patent medicine widely sold in North America.

I do not know whether Conan Doyle ever visited this continent, but it is possible that he might have seen the name in the advertising columns of American periodicals.

RAYMOND HULL
Haro Street, Vancouver,
Canada.

Daily Telegraph June 29 1955

LONDON DAY BY DAY
Holmes's diagnosis

I understand that at a recent spiritualist session the ghost of Mr. Sherlock Holmes, when asked how he accounted for the fact that there were now so many cars in the West End of London in spite of petrol rationing, replied:
"Supplementary, my dear Watson."

PETERBOROUGH

A BOOKMAN'S DIARY

The "birth" of Sherlock Holmes,
according to the calculations of
such redoubtable scholars as
Christopher Morley, occurred in
January, 1854, and all over the
world Sherlockians have been cele-
brating the centenary.

The flourishing Sherlock Holmes
Society of London held an anniversary dinner on January 14th. Its
members had been asked to disguise
themselves as Holmesian characters,
or to display articles associated
with the stories. Many of the diners
had followed up this suggestion,
and the impedimenta ranged from a
top hat to false whiskers, from a
butterfly net to a crutch.

As an uninitiated guest I found
all this slightly bewildering and my
perplexity changed to con-
sternation when my host quietly
produced a candle stump, a box of
matches — and a revolver. The
Sherlockians round me nodded
approval. "The Adventure of the
Three Garridebs," someone
murmured, "James Winter, alias
Morecroft alias Killer Evans, of
sinister and murderous
reputation . . ."
The revolver lay pointed towards
my plate throughout an excellent
dinner — naturally graced with
quantities of Beaune — and it was
still there when our chairman, Dr.
Maurice Campbell, rose to discourse
learnedly on the reasons for fixing
1954 as the Holmes centenary year.

Do Sherlockians take themselves
too seriously? Has the cult grown
to ridiculous proportions? The best
answer to that came from my
neighbour. "A little folly," he said,
"does nobody any harm."

The menu was, of course, printed
in Baskerville type.

Radio Times November 1954

'WHAT COMPANY, WATSON!'

In this month's B.B.C. radio production of "The Adventures of
Sherlock Holmes" John Gielgud is
to play Holmes with Ralph Richardson as Dr. Watson. The part of
Professor Moriarty will be taken
by Orson Welles.

Robin Jacques superb "Radio Times" illustration for "The Sign of the Four" broadcast as a play on B.B.C. Radio in February 1963.

Robin
Jacques

99

Stand in for Sherlock

Every now and again an envelope addressed to Sherlock Holmes, Esq., 221B Baker Street, finds its way to the Dead Letter Section of the G.P.O. in London. Whereupon those who deal with such matters smile indulgently and send it on to John Greaves.

Mr. Greaves, whose office stands where 221B would be if the street number existed, has become a kind of latter-day Dr. Watson, conscientiously answering Holmes' mail from all over the world.

It is a self-imposed task which he thoroughly enjoys — for already, as Secretary of the Dickens Fellowship, he finds that fictional characters are sometimes more vividly real to him than other people.

An amiable, comfortably rounded citizen who is resigned to being told that he looks just like Pickwick, he takes considerable pains over the replies which he dictates in his handsome fifth floor office, its bookcase stuffed with Dickens and Conan Doyle novels. Currently, he is rather pleased with the way he solved the problem put to him in a recent letter from Hamburg.

'Dear Mr. Holmes: it's known notorious that you have dissolved the heaviest criminal affairs on your writing table. I would enjoy very much to hear your

opinion about the disappearance of the frogman Crabb.'

Mr. Greaves, after some intensive research, came up with an answer which, he feels modestly, was not unworthy of Holmes himself.

'I feel sure after consulting the great detective's account of the mysterious affair of the Lion's Mane, that the disappearance of Crabb might well have been due to a similar cause, namely *Cyanea Capillata.*

'You will recollect if you have read this story that one man was killed and others seriously injured by a sea creature which resembled a lion's mane in the water . . . apparently it radiated invisible filaments to a distance of fifty feet which could sting a human being very severely and cause death.

'This occurred off the coast of Sussex, and no doubt when Sherlock Holmes destroyed the creature with a heavy rock parts of it broke off and survived along the coast. Hence the mysterious disappearance of the frogman.'

The first Holmes letter in Mr. Greaves bulging file arrived shortly after the end of the Sherlock Holmes exhibition held during the 1951 Festival of Britain. In the Abbey National building Holmes' famous sitting-room was reproduced in meticulous detail, from carpet slippers to pipe racks, deerstalker to magnifying glass. When the exhibition later went to the United States there was even a bottle of synthetic Baker Street fog.

Some of the letters are written in jest; some are earnest requests for information on the finer points of Holmesiana, from such societies as the Danish Baker Street Irregulars, the Speckled Band of Boston, and the Scandalous Bohemians of Akron. But most are sent to a detective who to the writers is a very real person. And Mr. Greaves is a man who hates to trample on an illusion.

Though he never replies as from Holmes, he carefully skates round the question of his existence; as in the case of eight-year-old Betsy Rusasco, of Indianapolis, who wrote:

'You're quite clever at solving cases. My sister and I play Sherlock Holmes but I have to be Watson. I know a man who has a pipe like yours. We have two long-haired dachshunds and when we play Sherlock Holmes we pretend they are bloodhounds. A magazine said you went to Indianapolis, U.S.A. Did you?' To which Mr. Greaves replied:

'Mr. Holmes had to vacate his flat and unfortunately I do not know his present address, so he may have gone to Indiana. I am sure he would have been most interested to hear about your games . . . Like you, I

Cover illustration for one of the numerous Holmes' pastiches "The Casebook of Solar Pons" (1965) by the late American Sherlockian enthusiast, August Derleth. Pons has been hailed by "Time" magazine as "the literary descendent of the Master" and appeared in some 57 adventures. Derleth set his stories in Praed Street, London and the detective has an assistant named Dr. Lyndon Parker. The publishing house which Derleth created especially for the Pons stories has the appropriate name of 'Mycroft & Moran'.

always enjoy reading stories of his adventures. Sorry I have no pictures showing his pipe, but I think you might like this one of him at work and also photographs of his sitting-room at 221B Baker Street. The majority of the letters come from the U.S.A., where a Sherlock Holmes series starring Basil Rathbone is widely shown on television; but they come, too, from most countries in Europe, from India and South America.

Mr. Greaves takes great trouble over letters from children, like the fourteen-year-old Brazilian who wrote: 'I am at your disposal in the defence of the good cause,' or the Italian youngster who asked: 'Will you be leaving for some punitive expedition against the Teddy Boys?' — and was sent the neatly typed reply: 'I feel sure that had Mr. Holmes been in practice at the present time he would certainly have been able to deal with them.'

Most optimistic, perhaps, was the Indian who wrote:

'As your hero-worshipper I present the enclosed Acrostic Anthem in honour of your hundredth birthday and shall appreciate of you mail your complete autobiography. The enclosed Acrostic may please be framed, to embalm it to posterity. Your reply will naturally be a great thrill of the century. Wishing you a glorious birthday with a red-litten sunrise . . .'

Mr. Greaves takes it all in his stride — even the occasional tourist who comes knocking at his door to see Sherlock Holmes in person. "I get used to it," he says, "and after all, the members of the Dickens Fellowship are a bit mad, too. We talk about Dickens' characters as though they were real people, and quite overlook the fact that they didn't live at all." As he wrote not long ago to the New Yorker who wanted to know the date of Holmes' death:

'I feel Sherlock Holmes never did die . . .'

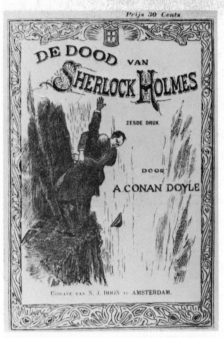

Above left: The word has gone around the world — and still does. One of the earliest Dutch editions of "The Adventures of Sherlock Holmes" from the turn of the century, and (right) a 1961 edition of "The Adventure of the Naval Treaty" and "The Adventure of Charles Augustus Milverton" in one volume.

The Sunday Times January 13 1957

THE ORIGINAL HOLMES BY IRVING WALLACE

Sir.— A recent letter from Mr. Adrian Conan Doyle has just been brought to my attention. In this letter, Mr. Doyle, having read Mr. Cyril Connolly's review of my book "The Fabulous Originals," strongly objects to a chapter in which I credit the remarkable Dr. Joseph Bell of Edinburgh as the prototype for Sherlock Holmes.

Mr. Doyle argues that his own father was the model for Sherlock Holmes — and that my attempt to award the honour to Dr. Bell is "a fairy tale."

While one must, indeed, admire Mr. Doyle's paternal devotion, one cannot help but feel that this very devotion detracts from his objectivity. I shall do no more than briefly summarise my case here.

1. The star witness in the case for Dr. Bell remains none other than the creator of Sherlock Holmes himself, Sir Arthur Conan Doyle, in a letter to Dr. Bell dated May 7, 1892, frankly acknowledged the source of his inspiration. He admitted that he owed the creation of Holmes to his old instructor's teachings and to his demonstrations of deduction, inference, and observation.

2. Over a period of years I corroborated Sir Arthur's admission by correspondence or personal interviews with other students who, like Doyle, had studied under Dr. Bell in the Royal Infirmary of Edinburgh and who knew the role their mentor played in the creation of Sherlock Holmes.

Even Robert Louis Stevenson, in 1893, after meeting the "ingenious and very interesting" Sherlock Holmes in print for the first time, asked Sir Arthur in a letter from Samoa: "Only one thing troubles me. Can this be my old friend Joe Bell?"

IRVING WALLACE
Los Angeles

The Daily Telegraph February 7 1958

HOLMES IN THE HOUSES OF PARLIAMENT

Once again, I see, that dog, over which Sherlock Holmes and Watson have their famous exchange in "Silver Blaze" has been trotted out — and slightly mishandled — on the floor of the House of Commons.

Mr. Hale, an assiduous reader with an exceptional memory, referred to it on Tuesday in the Tribunal debate. This was his version:

"Sherlock Holmes would have spoken of the strange conduct of the Lord Chancellor in the night-time. Dr. Watson would have said, 'The Lord Chancellor did not bark during the night-time or the day.' Sherlock Holmes would have replied that that was the strange conduct of the Lord Chancellor."

I am reminded of an earlier allusion. This was by Mr. Butler in October 1955 speaking in the autumn Budget. Twitting the Opposition with what they had not said in the General Election he remarked:

"It is rather like Sherlock Holmes and Dr. Watson; what was significant about the action of the dog? The dog did not bark."

Now the odd thing about this overworked quotation is that the word "bark" — included by Mr. Hale and Mr. Butler and many others — does not occur at all!

Here is the correct version:

"Is there any point to which you would wish to draw my attention?"

"To the curious incident of the dog in the night-time."

"The dog did nothing in the night-time."

"That was the curious incident," remarked Sherlock Holmes.

Aspiring politicians please copy.

PETERBOROUGH

"THE SPECKLED BAND" AT THE "ADELPHI"

MR A S HOMEWOOD AS THE TERRIFIED BUTLER!

MR LYN HARDING AS THE BAD, BAD, WICKED OLD MAN DR GRIMESBY RYLOTT

MISS CHRISTINE SILVER AS ENID

HOLMES' RIGHT HAND MAN!

"BILLY"

MARVELLOUS SIMPLY TERRIFIC!!

HOLMES FINDS A CLUE "AHA! JUST AS I THOUGHT! THE FLOOR IS NAILED TO THE BED!

SHERLOCK HOLMES IN A THINKING MOOD! (MR H A SAINTSBURY)

THE JURYMEN ARRIVE

The Great Detective on stage and screen

Mr. Sherlock Holmes, who loathed every form of society with his whole Bohemian soul, turned away with disdain from popular notoriety. It is not surprising therefore that he should have refused any part in the numerous dramatizations of his adventures on the stage and in the cinema.

That he would have made an excellent actor is undeniable. Dr. Watson has related many examples of his friend's amazing powers in the use of disguises and how his "expression, his manner, his very soul seemed to vary with every fresh part he assumed. The stage lost a fine actor, even as science lost an acute reasoner, when he became a specialist in crime."

Holmes himself admitted that he could never resist a touch of the dramatic and, at the denouement of *The Six Napoleons* when Watson and Lestrade "with a spontaneous impulse . . . broke out clapping as at the well-wrought crisis of a play," we are told that a "flush of colour sprang to Holmes's pale cheeks, and he bowed to us like the master dramatist who receives the homage of his audience." Unfortunately Mr. Holmes's powers as an actor were not displayed to the general public, so it remains to consider how he has been portrayed by professional actors on the stage and cinema screen.

The first author of a Holmes play appears to have been Charles Rogers, whose *Sherlock Holmes* was produced in Glasgow in May, 1894, with John Webb as Holmes and St. John Hammond as Watson. Little is known now of this play or its production.

Sir Arthur Conan Doyle, who had so brilliantly edited Watson's notes and presented them to a wider audience, entered the theatrical field in 1897 with a five-act drama, although, as he remarked in a letter, "I have grave doubts about putting Holmes on the stage at all." The play was sent to the impresario Charles Frohman, in New York. Frohman turned it over to the American actor-playwright William Gillette who undertook to rewrite it, having been given *carte blanche* in the selection of incidents and dialogue.

Gillette steeped himself in the Holmes stories and in four weeks produced his drama — so thoroughly rewritten that no one now knows what the original play was about. The only copy of the first draft was destroyed in an hotel fire, but a fortnight later Gillette had rewritten it yet again. *Sherlock Holmes,* this "absurd, preposterous, and thoroughly delightful melodrama," as it has been called, was an immediate success and it ran for 236 performances in New York. After a tour of America, it was brought to London in 1901 where it ran at the Lyceum for another 216 performances. (One of the early English actors in the

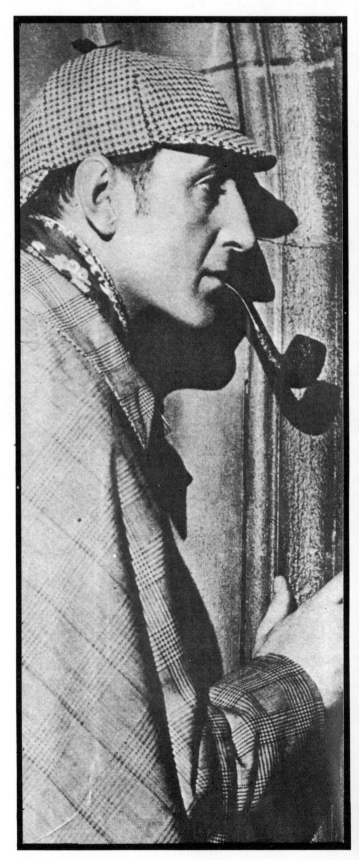

role of Billy, the pageboy, was Master Charles Chaplin.)

No small measure of the play's success was due to the performance of William Gillette in the title role — his physical appearance, temperament and personality have caused him to be revered by many as one of the greatest Holmeses of the footlights. Many other actors appeared in the title role during the numerous revivals, tours and translations of the play, but such was the attraction of Gillette that over thirty years after the original production he could still achieve a remarkable success with a farewell tour.

In 1910 Conan Doyle wrote a play version of *The Speckled Band*. It was produced at the Adelphi Theatre with H. A. Saintsbury as Holmes — a part he had already played over a thousand times on tour in Gillette's play — and Lyn Harding made an outstanding success as the formidable Dr. Rylott *[sic]*. Doyle was delighted and he has recorded in his memoirs that:

'We had a fine rock boa to play the title-role, a snake which was the pride of my heart . . . We had several snakes at different times, but they were none of them born actors and they were all inclined either to hang down from the hole in the wall like inanimate

Left: Basil Rathbone, one of the best Holmes, in "The Adventures of Sherlock Holmes" in 1940. Above: Clive Brook in "The Return of Sherlock Holmes" made in 1929. Right: A rare still from one of the earliest Holmes' films, "The Murder in Baker Street", made by the Nordisk Film Company of Denmark in 1908-12. The Great Detective is played by a German actor, Alwin Neuss.

Only a month after *Sherlock Holmes* had opened at the Lyceum, a popular burlesque appeared at Terry's Theatre in the Strand entitled *Sheerluck Jones* (or *Why D'Gillette Him Off?*), with Clarence Blakiston in the lead. This was followed three months later, in January, 1902, by John Lawson's *An Adventure in the Life of Sherlock Holmes*.

In America and in Europe about this period many unauthorized Holmes plays were produced. In Spain the popularity of the detective was enormous and he was pitted against celebrated criminals of fiction, such as Raffles and Arsene Lupin, in incredible adventures.

Another melodrama, entitled *Sherlock Holmes, Private Detective*, appeared in 1903, and 1905 saw the production of *The Bank of England: An Adventure in the Life of Sherlock Holmes*, by Max Goldberg. Also in 1905 came *The Painful Predicament of Sherlock Holmes*, a frivolous "curtain raiser" by William Gillette, who played Holmes, assisted by Charlie Chaplin as Billy and by Irene Vanbrugh.

bell-pulls, or else to turn back through the hole and get even with the stage carpenter who pinched their tails to make them more lively. Finally we used artificial snakes, and every one, including the stage carpenter, agreed that it was more satisfactory.'

The next production on the London stage was another play by Conan Doyle at the Coliseum in 1921 entitled *The Crown Diamond: An Evening with Sherlock Holmes*, with Dennis Neilson-Terry as Holmes. This one-act drama was not a success and Doyle adapted it into a short story under the title of *The Adventure of the Mazarin Stone*, which appeared in the *Strand Magazine* for October, 1921.

Two years later, Harold Terry and Arthur Rose collaborated in the writing of a melodrama, *The Return of Sherlock Holmes*, based upon the stories of *The Empty House* and *Lady Frances Carfax*. It had a long run at the Princes' Theatre, with Eille Norwood (who had just completed a brilliant series of forty-seven Holmes films) in the title role. In January, 1953, after a thorough revision by Arthur Rose and Ernest Dudley, the play was revived with great success at the New Theatre, Bromley. It was correctly set in the period of the 1890s and the most meticulous attention to the fine points of Holmesian detail was displayed by the producer, Stanley Van Beers.

The last play in this country, apart from revivals, was in 1933 at the Lyric Theatre, when Felix Aylmer and Sir Nigel Playfair appeared in *The Holmeses of Baker Street*, by Basil Mitchell. Thirty-four years previously Gillette had dared to show Holmes in love, but this amazing play revealed him as an elderly widower with a grown-up daughter! "When I have written to this man and told him that I hold him criminally responsible . . . we will have no more trouble," said Holmes in *The Creeping Man* — he must have taken similar action here, for the play was quickly

Between 1908 and 1910 the Nordisk Film Company of Denmark produced a series of thirteen film adventures, with such success that American, German and Italian film companies quickly followed suit and numerous cheap films with lurid plots appeared in the cinemas — one such masterpiece, *Sherlock Holmes in The Great Murder Mystery*, explained that "Holmes goes into a trance to pin a murder on an escaped gorilla — not based on Conan Doyle."

In 1912, however, the film rights were sold to the Eclair Company of France, who made nine films based on the original stories, and in 1914 *A Study in Scarlet*

withdrawn.

The views of Mr. Holmes upon his impersonators and their adventures in the cinema are, it is feared, like the case associated with the giant rat of Sumatra, "a story for which the world is not yet prepared." The earliest silent films may perhaps be excused, for the cinema was in its infancy, but it is difficult to resist applying Watson's graphic description of "ineffable twaddle" to many of the more recent versions — although the few exceptions were particularly memorable and outstanding.

It is believed that the earliest Holmes film was made in England about 1906, but no details can be traced.

was filmed in England, followed by *The Valley of Fear* in 1916. The same year saw an historic film version of the famous play *Sherlock Holmes*, made by Essanay and featuring William Gillette in his original role.

But a real turning point in the history of Holmes in the cinema was in 1921 when the Stoll Film Company of Great Britain released *The Adventures of Sherlock Holmes*, first of several series of extremely good films featuring Eille Norwood; forty-seven films were made in all. They were of a very high standard, sincere and, except for slight modernization, faithful to the original stories. Norwood's fine portrayal earned widespread praise and Doyle himself wrote: "He has that rare

quality which can only be described as glamour, which compels you to watch an actor eagerly when he is doing nothing. He has the brooding eye which excites expectation and he has also a quite unrivalled power of disguise."

One of the last silent films was *Moriarty* (American title: *Sherlock Holmes*) in 1922, starring John Barrymore and Roland Young. The character of Holmes was altered to suit Barrymore's more romantic personality and a prologue to the film dealt with Holmes's youth and college career.

The advent of the talking film was an occasion for prompt revival of interest in Sherlock Holmes, and between 1929 and 1939 many Holmes films were produced in England, America and on the Continent. However, only a few were of merit, although featuring well-known and accomplished actors. Notwithstanding that many of the films revealed glaring anachronisms and distortions of style and character, the principal fault lay in the fact that often the actor portraying Holmes lacked any physical resemblance to the established portrait, for this ethic of personal resemblance is an imperative requisite demanded by sentimental tradition.

The lineaments of Clive Brook are not really Holmesian, but in 1929 he impersonated the Great Man in *The Return of Sherlock Holmes*, and repeated the portrayal in *Sherlock Holmes* four years later. When Raymond Massey (*The Speckled Band*, 1931) and Robert Rendel (*The Hound of the Baskervilles*, 1932) essayed the role, enthusiasts groaned dismally at such violation of cherished tradition.

An example of muddled and misconceived casting gave Reginald Owen a curious claim to distinction, for

Above: Reginald Owen who had the unique distinction of playing both Holmes and Watson in two 1933 films. Middle: Carleton Hobbs and Norman Shelley, B.B.C. Radio's Holmes and Watson in 1959.

Right: A scene from another of the earliest Holmes' films, "A Study in Scarlet" made in 1914 by the Samuelson Film Company. The actor playing Holmes is unknown. (See page 118).

Below: The two most recent portrayers of Sherlock Holmes: Robert Stephens in the controversial "Private Lives of Sherlock Holmes" (1971) and Peter Cushing who has played the Master in both films and on television.

he is probably the only actor who has played both Holmes and Watson on the screen — in 1933 he was Watson to Clive Brook's Holmes, and later in the same year he was cast as Holmes in an unrecognizable version of *A Study in Scarlet.*

The year 1931, however, marked the debut of Arthur Wontner as Sherlock Holmes. In the prime of his distinguished career, Wontner gave a portrayal which is widely held to be the most authoritative. In the words of Vincent Starrett, doyen of Holmesian scholars, "no better Sherlock Holmes than Arthur Wontner is likely to be seen and heard in pictures, in our time. Sentimentalized, as is imperative, his detective is the veritable fathomer of Baker Street, in person. The keen, worn, kindly face and quiet, prescient smile are out of the very pages of the book." Lady Jean Conan Doyle in a letter to Mr. Wontner also expressed her delight in "your really splendid acting . . . [and] masterly personation of Sherlock Holmes."

The most recent well-known actor to portray Sherlock Holmes has been Basil Rathbone, who has appeared in fourteen films and over five hundred radio and television plays in America, at the end of last year he was seen on Broadway in *Sherlock Holmes,* a play written by his wife.

Rathbone's first Holmes film was an excellent version of *The Hound of the Baskervilles* in 1939. For the first time in film history the story was kept correctly in period and followed the original narrative fairly closely. Generally speaking, it was the best of all the Holmes films. A year later Rathbone appeared in *The Adventures of Sherlock Holmes,* another careful production in period, though by comparison less convincing.

It is somewhat astounding to recall the number of impersonations there have been. In the past sixty years some sixteen plays featuring Sherlock Holmes have been produced in England and America alone (it is impossible to estimate the countless revivals), whilst innumerable versions have appeared in other parts of the world. During the last forty-eight years Holmes has been portrayed in at least 115 films, and on the radio and television the number is well over a thousand.

Daily Express January 1 1958

Just fancy that

Sherlock Holmes went to court at Doncaster yesterday — to plead guilty to stealing coal worth £1 7s. from an open-cast coal site.

Holmes, A 37-year-old £15-a-week labourer, of Morton Road, Mexborough, was fined £5.

"A common loafer, with collar turned up, shiny, seedy coat, red cravat and worn boots." Eille Norwood as Holmes in disguise in "The Illustrious Client".

Daily Express September 15 1958

The case against Holmes by Moriarty

I cannot say how grieved I am at the insult paid to Mr. Sherlock Holmes by the uncouth persons who consider him to be old fashioned and worthy of no respect.

Sir, the memory of a desperate struggle on the edge of "a ghastly abyss" and of many other valiant ventures, has convinced me that Holmes, Englishman though he be, is no fuddy-duddy.

PROFESSOR MORIARITY
(Charles Milverton)
Rosslyn Hill, Hampstead, N.W.

Note: Inside Show Business (Thursday) reported that the British company remaking the Hound of the Baskervilles will not mention Sherlock Holmes in advertising the picture because "teenagers think him a fuddy-duddy."

Daily Express November 12 1958

3-D? IT'S ELEMENTARY, MY DEAR WATSON
By JAMES THOMAS

The B.B.C. will broadcast its first 3-D sound radio play on Saturday — a 25-minute production starring Sherlock Holmes.

The play will be part of the B.B.C.'s experimental stereophonic relay between 10.15 and 11.15 on Saturday morning.

The producer, Raymond Raikes, said yesterday: "These scenes from 'Sherlock Holmes' are only a beginning.

"But listen for such things as the knife whizzing right across the room, the passing hansom cab, the sound of Holmes's violin at one end of his study as Watson enters through the door at the other."

The relay can be picked up by positioning a TV set and radio six feet apart. Half the transmission will come through the TV speaker, the other half through the radio on the Third Programme channel.

Soon the B.B.C. will be experimenting with a new kind of "solid sound" which can be transmitted over one modified aerial instead of through two stations. But anyone who wants to pick up will have to have a special radio set and an extension speaker.

LITTLE CARTOON
By BERNARD HOLLOWOOD
Editor of "Punch"

(Conan Doyle was born 100 years ago.)

10.30 THE PUBLIC LIFE OF

SHERLOCK HOLMES

A case-book of Sherlockiana to celebrate the centenary of Holmes's creator, Sir Arthur Conan Doyle (born May 22, 1859) Introduced by Leonard Maguire

Linking script by Eddie Boyd Compiled and produced by W. Gordon Smith

Radio Times May 15 1959

John O'London's December 3 1959

THE BELL THAT DIDN'T RING

In Mr. A. G. Thornton's witty article 'The Bell That Didn't Ring' in your issue of December 3, the author says: "Sherlock Holmes knew of the existence of the telephone but he never used it."

Now, if Mr. Thornton had read the entire *Saga*, he would have known that in two Holmes-cases ('The Three Garridebs' and the 'Retired Colourman') the telephone played its part and was actually installed at 221B Baker Street. True, this was during the last years of Holmes's practice as a consulting detective.

Cornelis Herring,
President, The Dutch Sherlock Holmes Society,
W. de Zwijgerlaan 115, Amsterdam.

The Daily Telegraph December 13
1957

THE SHERLOCK HOLMES INN WHERE BASKERVILLE LOST A BOOT

Sherlock Holmes, whose records show he was not averse to an occasional mild tipple in between bouts of sleuthing, was given another manifest of immortality yesterday.

The old Northumberland Arms public house, in Northumberland Street, near Charing Cross Station, near Inspector Lestrade of the Yard and Sir Henry Baskerville, whose hound needs no introduction, was formally reopened as The Sherlock Holmes.

Part of the Sherlock Holmes Festival of Britain exhibition, curved pipe, stale toast, hypodermic syringe and all, has been exported from Baker Street to Northumberland Street for a nearly complete reproduction of Mrs. Hudson's sitting-room. It occupies part of the new grill-room.

"Doesn't make sense," said one of the waitresses. "With a snack bar I could make £5 a week clear on that bit of space."

Brown boot clue

Mr. H. Douglas Thomson, a director of Whitbread and Co., to appease Baker Stret Irregulars and Holmesian societies at home and abroad, explained that it would have been ideal to have had a Sherlock Holmes pub in Baker Street. But this was not possible.

On the other hand Holmes and Dr. Watson, it was more than evident, had more than one pint of bitter beer in the original Northumberland Hotel and crossed the street for Turkish baths to repair whatever was called a hangover in those days.

Mortgage deeds were on show to prove that the newly-named public house formed part of the hotel where Sir Henry Baskerville lost a brown boot and found for Holmes the clue which led the trail of the Hound of the Baskervilles.

Even the 52-page catalogue of Holmesiana adorning the premises was set in Baskerville type.

Holmes was invited

Holmes was invited to the lunch-time opening. Latest reliable reports are that he is a busy bee-keeper in Sussex. Characteristically, he sent no quotable response to the invitation.

It was thought probably that he is deeply engaged on a monograph on "The Hibernation Habits of the Hive, and the essential analysis of Sussex wild flower pollen as an aid to crime detection."

Nor was there any word from Dr. Watson. His dissatisfaction with the National Health Service is believed to have led to a temporary return to the North-West Frontier.

Mrs. Hudson, now in retirement has made it known for a long time that, with respect, she is too old for such goings on.

Whether Inspector Lestrade was there or not is not known. Out of deference to Scotland Yard colleagues who have spent more time at the old Northumberland Arms than he ever spent at 221B, Baker Street, it was authoritatively stated he preferred to remain incognito among the War Office clerks and local office workers who have used the house for years.

Yesterday they contemplated with true British phlegm the prospect of becoming a new tourist attraction in London.

WHITBREAD

SHERLOCK HOLMES

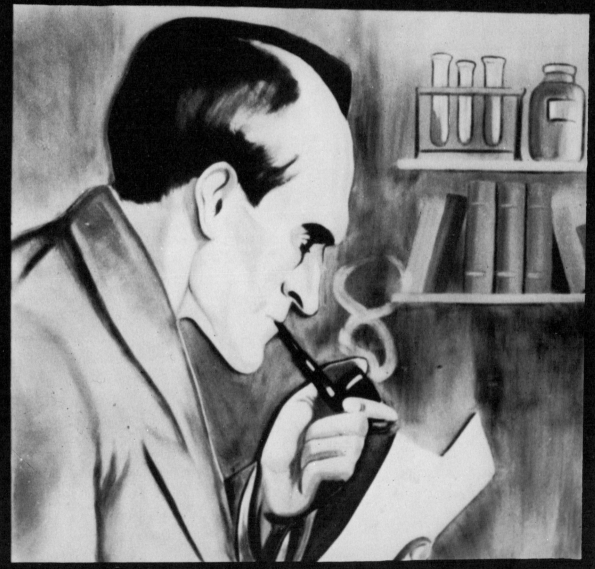

The Sunday Telegraph June 25 1961

DEAR, DEAR WATSON
BY DEREK BOWMAN

Except for his admiration for the one woman who got the better of him, Sherlock Holmes never paid much attention to the opposite sex. What he would have made of a female Dr. Watson is hard to imagine — but a female Dr. Watson appears in Joan Littlewood's newest production, "They Might Be Giants," at the Theatre Workshop, Stratford, E., on Wednesday.

The real Holmes, of course, would never tolerate such a thing, but the explanation is simple. The play is about an American ex-judge called Playfair (Harry H. Corbett) who goes mad and imagines he is the Great Detective. Dr. Mildred Watson (Avis Bunnage) is his psycho-analyst.

The author who has had the temerity to put Sherlock Holmes — even a phoney one — into an American love story is a 33-year-old Chicagoan, James Goldman, who looks like a younger brother of Arthur Miller. It is his first play to be produced, and it took him two years to write in a New York apartment. He sent it to the impresarios, the late Robert E. Griffith and Harold Prince, who decided that only Miss Littlewood could do it justice.

"My madman is very verbal. He has no trouble talking," says the taciturn Mr. Goldman.

"As well as being a love story it's a detective story and deals with upper class characters in New York — though there will be no American accents used.

"The play attempts to say a number of things connected with our assessment of the world around us. It asks us to look much more imaginatively and deeply at things we take for granted."

All very well, of course, but Sherlock Holmes enthusiasts are serious people: what will they say about an American fake Holmes and a female Watson in a comedy which ends up with its 30 characters in a wild chase across the stage?

"No offence is meant and I hope none is taken. Playfair is after Professor Moriarty just as Holmes is," says Mr. Goldman.

The Times September 14 1959

THE CASE OF THE PREDETERMINED GAME
Holmes & Watson at the Tourists' Match
Leeds 20 pts, Australians 44

"Watson, pray open the sealed envelope I entrusted to your care on Saturday morning. It contains a prediction that the Australian Rugby League team would defeat Leeds by a substantial margin; further, that they would score most of their points in the second half."

"Amazing, Holmes."

"Elementary, my dear Watson. If you have bent up your mind to absorb the facts of current football, you will know that Leeds are now but a shadow of other teams they have had in recent years. With your limited powers of observation you may also have discovered that this was their fourth match in eight days. In this extraordinary weather, my dear Watson, the inflexible surface of the earth has an unfortunate effect upon such human frames as are thrown violently upon it. At Leeds, as elsewhere, there are men temporarily *hors de combat.*

"The Australians, on the other hand, were playing their first match in this country. They are out-rageously fit young men who run with uncommon celerity. All this you may, with application, have learned from your newspaper. And though your mind is not unduly retentive, you must be aware that fast runners prefer hard ground. In all these circumstances my prediction was inevitable.

"Come, my dear Watson, we may safely leave the details to the newspapers. Weightier matters await our attention."

Advertisement for the "Strand Magazine" placed in the national newspapers in January 1949. Sadly, the periodical was already doomed and was finally incorporated into "Men Only" in March 1950.

LET'S FACE IT! By Lewis Williams

"Yes, comrade—I DO have a theory about the popularity of Sherlock Holmes in Russia, but I hesitate to mention it!"

The Daily Telegraph August 18 1959

CONAN DOYLE SUIT FAILS
Moscow courts payment bar
From a special correspondent
MOSCOW, Monday

Sherlock Holmes suffered one of his rare defeats here to-day, as did the hundreds of Western authors who were looking over his shoulder in the fight for authors' compensation from Soviet publishers.

The Supreme Court of the Russian Federation upheld a lower court's ruling that foreign writers were not entitled to royalties or other compensation from the sale of their works in the Soviet Union.

The decision left the matter of authors' rights where it has been since the Communists seized power in 1917. Soviet publishing houses are free to publish any work of any writer whose country has not made a special agreement with Moscow to cover his rights.

They may, and in a few cases do, pay royalties to the authors, but they are not obliged to do so. The legal basis for this is a section of the Soviet copyright law which specifically exempts foreign authors from its protection.

Efforts to challenge it have failed repeatedly. The Supreme Court held to-day that a complaint brought by the estate of Sir Arthur Conan Doyle was merely an attempt to circumvent this exemption and therefore inadmissible.

Sir Arthur's son, Adrian, and his counsel, Prof. Harold J. Berman, of Harvard University, thought they had found a legally plausible and politically palatable way of obtaining compensation.

They conceded that they had no claim for royalties, but argued that, under a clause of the Russian Re-public's' civil code forbidding "unjust enrichment," they were entitled to a share of the profits from sale of Sir Arthur's books.

Prof. Berman estimated that the defendants, the Ministry of Culture, and four publishing houses, had had a gross income of 13,555,850 roubles (about £1¼ million at the normal rate) from Conan Doyle's books sold before May 1, 1957. Putting the author's fair share at 15 per cent., they claimed compensation of 2,033,347 roubles (about £180,000).

Had he won his case Prof. Berman would have filed also for a share of receipts from the sale of another 11 million copies of the Sherlock Holmes stories since May, 1957. He had also offered to accept a share of profits instead of a flat 15 per cent.

The suit was dismissed last year by Moscow City Court. The claimants could request the Procurator to ask for another review by Supreme Court of the Soviet Union, but they have decided not to press the case further.

Cover of one of the unauthorised Russian translations of "The Adventures of the Six Napoleons" published in Moscow in 1945.

The appeal was heard in a small room in the Supreme Court building a few blocks from the Kremlin. The room was simply furnished.

In high-backed chairs decorated with hammers and sickles, sat three judges. Prof. Berman said he had been unable to get Soviet legal assistance and presented his case in Russian with only occasional assistance from an interpreter.

Anna D. Nescheglotova, an assistant Procurator, took only five minutes to urge rejection of the plea. The defendants were not directly represented.

Beside Western correspondents, there were only five interested Soviet citizens present, including lawyers. They listened attentively to Professor Berman's argument, but left before the decision, confident of the outcome.

As is customary in cases of procedure here, no stenographic or other record was kept of the hearing. Thus, as the case was not accepted for trial, it will not go into the records.

For the same reason the Conan Doyle estate will not have to pay the normal fee levied against losers in Soviet civil cases — six per cent of the sum claimed.

The Sunday Times 16 April 1967

PERSONAL

HOLMES, arrived Syon Lodge, Isleworth, Middlesex. Signs of recent struggles. Thousands of antiques in mansion and grounds but can detect nothing spurious. Mr. Crowther opens 7 days a week: states struggles all occasioned by clients fighting impulse to purchase. Returning tomorrow; please accept delivery at Baker Street of Chippendale chimneypiece on my behalf. WATSON.

Daily Express March 19 1965

The women in Sherlock's life

Love never found a way with Sherlock Holmes. Yet the super-sleuth of Baker Street created half a century ago by Arthur Conan Doyle — his adventures are all crime, no sex — is having a remarkable revival on both sides of the Atlantic.

The musical "Baker Street" is a hit on Broadway. In Britain, the B.B.C.-TV series, "Sherlock Holmes," plays to an audience of more than 11 million every Saturday night, it was announced yesterday.

The 12 episodes are costing £60,000, and American TV companies are showing interest in buying it.

No Kissing

What is new about Sherlock Holmes? Just that he is the half-forgotten original of all the private-eyes, ace detectives, and thriller heroes of our era.

A sign outside the New York theatre showing "Baker Street" says: "Sherlock Holmes taught James Bond all he knows!"

Except, of course, that Sherlock Holmes knew next to nothing about women. He never admired a pretty ankle, or kissed a fragrant female cheek.

The American musical tries to inject romance into the Sherlock Holmes story by involving him with the celebrated Irene Adler, the only woman who achieves any prominence in the Holmes saga.

Unusual

Miss Adler (according to the story) was an operatic contralto, born in New Jersey, and sometime good friend of the King of Bohemia.

"She is the daintiest thing under a bonnet on this planet," remarked Sherlock Holmes once.

For the hawk-nosed detective in the deerstalker hat, this was an unusually fulsome, almost gushing, thing to say about a member of the opposite sex.

But the affair went no further, of course. Mr. Colin Prestige, a London solicitor and secretary of the Sherlock Holmes Society, told me: "The idea of the Great Detective actually becoming involved in a romance with Miss Adler is quite, quite ridiculous. Holmes didn't do that kind of thing."

A bachelor, firmly attached to his briar pipe and spy-glass, Holmes had only one true friend — Dr. Watson, of course.

Watson worried about Holmes.

Two versions of the delectable Mary Morstan. Opposite page: As portrayed by Isobel Elson with Eille Norwood in "The Sign of Four" in 1923 and Above: as seen by an unknown artist in "Stories of Sherlock Holmes" published in America by Harpers in 1904. Left: Basil Rathbone with the beautiful Ida Lupino in "The Adventures of Sherlock Holmes" (1940) and Below: Inga Swenson as Irene Adler has designs on Sherlock (Fritz Weaver) in the American Stage musical, "Baker Street" (1965).

"No wonder, he was a classic manic-depressive," said actor Douglas Wilmer, who read everything he could find about Holmes before accepted the leading role in the TV series.

"He was rude, dedicated, disagreeable, ruthless, passionate — and peculiar. Those heroin-induced glooms couldn't be normal, could they?"

Dr. Watson wanted to see Holmes married and settled. But even the atrractive Miss Violet Hunter — "a woman with a mind," said Holmes — could not distract him from the riddle in hand.

Cynical

"I'm engaged!" announced the great detective one day. Dr. Watson beamed with pleasure. Disguised as a plumber, Holmes had promised marriage to a Hampstead housemaid.

But, of course, there was no love in it. Holmes was following up a few clues, and cynically trifled with the maid's affections in order to get on the inside track.

Perhaps the Sherlock Holmes revival will start a new fashion in heroes — the crime-buster who cares more about the crime than he does about busts.

Evening Mail June 12 1965

THE CASE OF THE UNKNOWN HOLMES
BY ARTHUR STEELE

Who was the man in the deerstalker hat, sucking a pipe with rather soulful expression which was no doubt meant to indicate that Sherlock Holmes was engaged in a particularly baffling mystery?

All we know is that he was an accountant in a Birmingham film office.

And he was chosen to play the great detective in the first in which Holmes appeared.

That alone should earn him a place in cinema annals. But no one knows his name.

With Sherlock Holmes riding a fresh wave of popularity — new Holmes films are now being shot, and the musical, "Baker Street" is breaking records on Broadway — the identification of the first in the long, long line of his movie interpreters would be particularly satisfying to all Holmes fans.

And particularly to Mr. Michael Pointer, of Grantham, who has sent me details of his own efforts to solve this particular mystery. It is a detection story in its own right.

After years spent, with a colleague, in cataloguing all the data on Holmes plays and films which they could track down, Mr. Pointer admits that, unlike the unique character whom Conan Doyle created, he accepts defeat. Unless the readers of this column can help.

The film was a 1914 version of "A Study in Scarlet." It was the first story into which Conan Doyle brought his apparently deathless detective.

And it was the first picture to be made by the Samuelson Film Company. It was shot at Worton Hall, Isleworth, and produced by one of the British movie pioneers, George Pearson.

It featured Fred Paul and Agnes Glynne. Beyond that Mr. Pointer could at first find nothing.

With the discovery of a book by Mr. Pearson, the producer, he was back on the trail.

In it was an account of "A Study in Scarlet."

After details of shooting in Cheddar Gorge and on Southport sands (for the Rockies and the plains of Salt Lake), Mr. Pearson went on: "Sherlock Holmes was a problem. Much depended on his physical appearance. Build, height, mannerisms had to be correct.

"By a remarkable stroke of fortune G. B. Samuelson had an employee in his Birmingham office who absolutely fitted these requirements . . . I decided to risk his engagement as the shrewd detective.

"With his long and lean figure, his deer-stalker hat, cape-coat and curved pipe, he looked the part and played the part excellently."

But still no name.

The trail now looked promising. Mr. George Pearson was eventually reached by letter.

But he had no record of the man who had played Holmes.

All he recalled was that the man was the accountant at Samuelson's Royal Film Agency in Corporation Street.

The trail turned to the British Film Institute, to which Mr. Pearson said he had given a number of stills from the film.

And that is where the portrait of the unknown Holmes was found. And where the trail flickered out.

The identify of the non-professional actor of 50 years ago still remains one unsolved mystery in the history of Holmes.

Radio Times January 18 1962

The Voice of Holmes

My dear rather silly old grandfather always used to recall meeting Holmes in his prime year of 1895, and being addressed by him thus: 'Woodman's Lee, cabby, as quick as you can go!'

The tones in which this thrilling command was uttered he always described as 'high and somewhat strident,' the very term used by Watson of his friend's voice in "The Stockbroker's Clerk."

Highly strident leading players are little favoured by modern audiences. What might be termed 'astringency' of voice is a good microphone substitute; and if ever there was an astringent voice it is surely that of Carleton Hobbs, whose portrayal, according to numerous listeners, epitomise the Sherlock Holmes of their imagination.

MICHAEL HARDWICK
London, W.1.

Daily Express October 2 1968

ROBERT PITMAN
In my opinion

Though no Baker Street fanatic, I rejoice that the new television "Hound of the Baskervilles" is so authentic and so much better than the earlier efforts in the series.

In 1960 we took a really cheap (£15 a head) family trip to Leningrad. Without the aid of guides, we discovered that, despite the myth, almost no Russian speaks a second language.

But one bright-eyed boy of 12 did. He prattled at us. He cried: "Sherlock Holmes!" "Baskerville dog!" "Woof, woof!" It was, obviously, one of his favourite school books.

We have often smiled at the memory of the Baskerville dog. But now we find ourselves wondering about that happy, genial boy.

Where are you, little Ivan? Are you lining up bravely with those other young radicals in defence of free speech against the Kremlin?

Or are you perhaps strutting in boots around Prague, with all the solidity of Dr. Watson and without a particle of his kindliness and conscience?

The Daily Telegraph March 19 1970

LONDON DAY BY DAY
In Holmes's footsteps

Sherlock Holmes's association with Baker Street began in 1887, but not until now has it become visible. Today a "My Dear Watson" coffee shop opens there and in the summer a 160-bedroom hotel named after the detective, on the site of the former YWCA headquarters.

This project is welcomed by the Sherlock Holmes Society of London and two of its members, Michael and Mollie Hardwick, who have written five books about Conan Doyle's creation and dramatised many of the stories, are helping the hotel with its atmosphere.

They are also assisting a Knightsbridge travel agency to set up tours of the south and west "in Holmes's footsteps."

IT APPEARS THAT OUR QUARRY HAS VANISHED WATSON!

Three modern strip cartoons featuring the Immortal Detective. Top: "The Red-Headed League" from the London "Evening Standard." Middle: "The Sussex Vampire" from the American "Washington Post" and Bottom: "The Black Death" from the French "France Soir" (1954-5).

UP WITH YOUR HANDS!

FRANK GIACOIA 4-18

DON'T SHOOT, LESTRADE! YOU'LL HIT WATSON!

THEY'VE BOTH SCURRIED BACK INTO THEIR TUNNEL!

I'M GOING IN AFTER THEM!

SIR ARTHUR CONAN DOYLE

BE QUICK, MR. HOLMES! THAT DART IS POISONED!

FRANK GIACOIA 8-1

HURRY! SUCK THE WOUND TO GET THE POISON OUT!

SIR ARTHUR CONAN DOYLE

Holmes, je soupçonne qu'on veut nous signifier que nous ne devons pas entrer au château!

Vous méritez un bon point, Watson!

Comme vous le voyez, M. Holmes, c'est la seule entrée du château!

Et voici la seule clé qui ouvre cette porte!

Et c'est ici que vous vous trouviez avec Miss Emily, M. Jelliby, quand vous avez entendu le coup de feu qui a tué M. Joad?

Pas moi, M. Holmes, je suis un peu sourd et n'ai entendu que cet infernal ressac. C'EST EMILY qui me l'a dit!

By the Reichenbach Falls

Two famous views of the grim battle between Holmes and Professor Moriarty in May 1891 which seemingly resulted in the death of the Great Detective — until public pressure caused Conan Doyle to re-suscitate him. Above: Arthur Twidle's illustration for the 1903 edition of "The Memoirs of Sherlock Holmes"; and Right: Sidney Paget's original interpretation for the "Strand Magazine" (December 1893). This event has proved the inspiration for innumerable newspaper reports over the years, not the least of these being a "Times" Leader of August 1966. Two years later, in May 1968, members of the London Sherlock Holmes Society decided to mark the event with a special 'pilgrimage' to the scene where two members re-enacted the death struggle. The event was recorded in inventive style by the "Daily Sketch's" reporter, Frederick Newman (see overleaf).

Day after day this summer has come news of tragedy in the Alps. Men of great experience who have lived all their lives among the mountains have been killed as well as newcomers from outside. Yesterday there was a fresh variant on this grim theme. One of the smugglers who operate across the frontier between Italy and Switzerland was making his way with three of his companions, pack on back, along a narrow path by the edge of a ravine. A customs official was on their trail. The smuggler slipped, the customs man grabbed at him, and both fell into the ravine.

For an English audience this sad story of human hunter and hunted in the Alps has one inevitable echo. The date is May 4, 1891; the place the Reichenbach Falls. From London to Switzerland Holmes and Watson have been dodging Professor Moriarty. They have given him the slip in Belgium and France, and gone by the Gemmi Pass and Interlaken to the little village of Meiringen. There they have put up at the English Hof. Thence they have taken their fatal detour to admire the Falls, and together stood "near the edge peering down at the gleam of the breaking water far below." And there, a few hours later, the great detective and the Napoleon of crime end their contest, reeling over the abyss, locked in each other's arms.

But of course only one of them really reeled. Holmes's return to life three years later is still one of the most dramatic and controversial passages in literature. It was responsible for the only recorded occasion on which Watson fainted. And who should blame him? Even though Watson was used to Holmes's disguises (had he not been a decrepit Italian priest for part of the journey which led to Meiringen?) it was a bit thick to reappear in Watson's rooms as an even more decrepit bookseller, and thicker still to throw off the disguise without warning.

The Final Problem, which brought Holmes and Moriarty to their fatal confrontation, was so apparently conclusive that to this day there are many who find Holmes's explanation of how he escaped unsatisfactory. Father Knox distinguished between those international scholars who thought Watson had faked The Final Problem for his own purposes, and those who "regard The Final Problem as genuine and the Return-stories as a fabrication". The evidence of the latter is not easily disposed of ("The true Holmes never splits an infinitive; the Holmes of the Return-stories splits at least three", and so on). And yet if such stories as The Norwood Builder and The Dancing Men do not belong to the true canon, what is anyone to think? Conan Doyle himself described them as bulls-eyes. He ought to know.

A pictorial likeness, made by Mr. Geoffrey White of the London Daily Sketch, of Mr. Holmes and Prof. Moriarty locked in combat.

PRESUMED DEATH OF Mr SHERLOCK HOLMES

Tragic Occurrence As The Detective Plunges From Precipitous Ledge

---

PROF. MORIARTY ALSO PERISHES

From Our Own Correspondent, Mr FREDERICK NEWMAN. MEIRINGEN, May 1st.

I MUST confess it was not entirely by chance that I found myself today upon the mountainside 2,400 ft. above Meiringen. In truth, rumour and speculation concerning extraordinary circumstances had drawn me there.

Even so, I was scarcely prepared for the spectacle that met my eyes. Before me, balanced on the edge of a fearful abyss, were two elderly persons – one in deer-stalker and cape, the other in a black frock coat – who by their garb I took to be gentlemen.

Yet by their actions, their grunting and snarling, their grappling with each other, and their evident determination to hurl each other from the perilous ledge on which they perched, they appeared far from refined.

Touching first one and then the other lightly upon the shoulder with my cane, I addressed myself to each in turn above the roar of the Reichenbach Falls behind them.

"Pray excuse me," I begged as the falls tumbled 600 ft. in clouds of spray. "But what is the meaning of this curious performance?"

The figure in the cape, whom, upon closer inspection, I perceived to possess a fine, aquiline nose and powerful, bush-like eyebrows, declared that he was Sir Paul Gore-Booth, head of the Diplomatic Service – a fact which I was at first disinclined to believe, but was able later to confirm.

"I am playing the part of Sherlock Holmes," he replied courteously enough, though in a somewhat breathless manner. "And I am re-enacting the death struggle between Holmes and that arch criminal Moriarty, which took place at the very falls on May 4, 1891."

"Then this," I said, turning to Sir Paul's antagonist and entering into the spirit of the matter. "I deduce to be Professor Moriarty."

MULTITUDE

He replied: "Quite so, but shortly I shall be the late Prof. Moriarty, whereupon I shall be once more Mr. Charles Scholefield, QC, Barrister and Master of the Middle Temple."

I observed that the two men were well matched: Sir Paul, 59 years old and six foot tall; Prof. Moriarty, aged 66 and 6ft. 4in., and not more than a few pounds between them.

At the same time, I could not but notice that their efforts stemmed not from any bitter emnity towards each other, but were rather directed towards the satisfaction of a great multiude of camera-operators, who hung like bats from the surrounding rocks.

I gathered that Sir Paul is President, and Mr. Scholefield a member of the Sherlock Holmes Society, which has inspired this pilgrimage to Meirengen as the climax to a tour of Switzerland, during which scenes of many of Holmes' adventures here have been revisited.

Having struggled manfully for some minutes, and with Sir Paul confessing that at the Foreign Office he was more accustomed to wrestling of a more intellectual nature, the two men fell apart. Somewhat thankfully, it occurred to me.

SCREAMING

Now their places were taken by two similarly dressed Alpine guides who with bloodcurling yodels and a great deal of tottering and tumbling rolled on the brink of the Reichenbach Falls in the very place described by Holmes's creator, Sir Arthur Conan Doyle.

Two photographic likenesses of Sir Paul and Mr. Scholefield had been despatched from London by Special Courier, and from these the guides had prepared effigies.

Amid gasping and screaming and groaning and hissing from 40 odd watching members of the Sherlock Holmes Society, these effigies were now observed to plunge into the cauldron of the falls.

There seemed no doubt but that Moriarty was dead, and few will weep for this treacherous blackguard. But had Holmes, the greatest detective that ever lived, died too?

The sunlight continued to pierce the rising sprays of the falls. The heavens did not darken. Portents, surely, that Holmes had not expired?

Take comfort, dear reader, Holmes re-appeared this very afternoon while a dignitary of Meirengen was delivering his funeral oration.

PRIVILEGES

And the great man learned into the bargain that he had been made an honorary citizen of the village. Should he pass this way again, he will be entitled, among other privileges to free use of the toilets at Meirengen Railway Station.

Miraculously, Holmes is still alive, a sturdy 140-year-old.

It would be a mystery, indeed, were he allowed to die.

NOT BEFORE THE PUBLIC!
BY POLLY TOYNBEE

Dedicated members of the Sherlock Holmes Society of London are outraged by the new film called 'The Private Life of Sherlock Holmes.'

One scene suggests that Holmes and Watson were a homosexual couple. Mr Philip Dalton, the society's secretary, commented yesterday, 'The idea is fantastic. I think it is rather revolting.'

Lord Gore-Booth, the former head of the Foreign Office, who played the part of the great detective when the society made a fancy-dress pilgrimage to Switzerland in 1968, said yesterday: 'I reacted to the film rather as Shakespeare would have reacted if he had seen the play "Rosencrantz and Guildenstern are Dead." Nothing in the stories suggests that Holmes was homosexual. I think this is quite out of the spirit of Conan Doyle.'

But what about Holmes's brother Mycroft, member of the Misogynists Clyb? 'He was just a clever, lazy, clubman. It's a very fashionable interpretation.'

Civil servant James Holroyd, a Holmesian expert who has published two books on the subject, 'Baker Street Byways,' and 'Seventeen Steps to 221B,' said: 'There is no suggestion whatever of homosexuality in the stories. In fact, there is fairly conclusive evidence that Watson had three different wives, and at the end of "The Sign of Four" he falls in love.'

Barrister Anthony Hallet said: 'As a Sherlock Holmes story the film didn't even begin. I suppose the good looks of Robert Stephens (who plays the name part) would appeal to the ladies, but he behaved absolutely abominably to his housekeeper, Mrs Hudson.'

Mr Hallet agreed that occasionally the society had debated the question of Holmes's sex life. 'We played around with the idea, twisting quotations and taking them out of context, but that was only for our own amusement. We'd never do it in public.'

The new faces of Holmes! Since the death of Sir Arthur Conan Doyle there have been several sequels to the Adventures, some of the best being by his son, Adrian. The scene here was drawn by Robert Fawcett for Adrian's "The Adventure of the Red Window" which appeared in "Collier's" in 1953. Another tale which he wrote with John Dickson Carr, "The New Exploits of Sherlock Holmes" prompted Professor Moriarty to emerge from the shadows to pen the letter here to the London "Evening Standard" in October 1953. Perhaps the most controversial of the new interpretations of Holmes has been the film, "The Private Lives of Sherlock Holmes" made by Billy Wilder in 1970. In the scene here Holmes, played by Robert Stephens, is being kissed by Genevieve Page, while an astounded Dr. Watson (Colin Blakeley) looks on. Sherlock also obviously has a place far into the future as this cover illustration for "The Science-Fictional Sherlock Holmes" shows. Published in 1960 by American enthusiasts, the book took the Great Detective and Dr. Watson on exploits into the far reaches of the universe.

Daily Express January 3 1973

BANK RAID 'COPY OF 1890 STORY'
BY ARNOLD LATCHAM

The 1971 Great Bank Robbery was a "dead ringer" of one of Sherlock Holmes's most famous cases.

It took place 16 months ago only a stone's throw from Mr. Holmes's legendary lodgings in Baker Street, London.

And it was a real life copy of a crime in June, 1890, described in the Sherlock Holmes story "The Redheaded League," said prosecutor Mr. Robert Harman at the Old Bailey yesterday.

Deftly to a jury of ten men and two women, Mr. Harman compared the robberies of fact and fiction, and the one vital difference between them.

In **Fiction** the robbers tunnelled their way to the bank vaults from two doors away and when they came up through the floor found Mr. Holmes, Dr. Watson, and the bank manager waiting for them.

In **Fact** when the 1971 robbers did exactly the same thing — tunnelling into Lloyds Bank Baker Street branch from a shop also two doors away — there was no one waiting for them.

"So," said Mr. Harman, "they got clean away with money and safety deposit valuables in excess of £1½ million."

An added clue to the 1971 raid was revealed by Mr. Harman as he described how the gang got to know the layout.

One of the thieves, 37-year-old Reginald Tucker, rented a safety deposit which enabled him regularly to visit the bank vaults and measure them up roughtly with his umbrella.

Mr. Harman said the raiders came up into the bank on the weekend of September 11, 1971, through a 7ft. by 5ft. hole.

Their starting point was an empty shop 40 yards away.

And, said Mr. Harman, the tunnel they used was so perfectly excavated by 38-year-old photographer Anthony Gavin that it did not need any props to keep the roof up.

Mr. Harman added that all the equipment for the job was provided by 35-year-old car dealer Thomas Stephens.

Stephens of Maygood Street, Islington; Tucker of Lee Street, Hackney; and Gavin of Brownlow Road, Dalston, have pleaded guilty to stealing from the bank and possessing explosives. They await sentence.

Daily Telegraph April 5 1973

"Hurry up! They still believe we are re-enacting an old Sherlock Holmes adventure!" Bill Tidy's "Punch" cartoon of May 1968 seems an amazing premonition of the news story.

ELEMENTARY

At a recent Yugoslav book trade meeting, President Tito condemned the import and publication of "pornography and trashy literature." But he praised Sherlock Holmes. "As a child," he said, "I read books about Sherlock Holmes. I think that such books can develop children's imagination and sense of justice."

With unexpected frankness Tito called Marx's works "the heaviest kind of literature, making great demands on time and concentration." He suggested that the way to encourage people to read them was to produce popular editions.

Even better (and incidentally reconciling an inherent contradiction) would be to produce books in which Marx and his teachings were merged with the life and philosophy of Sherlock Holmes, with Fred Engels at his side, perhaps, as a fox-hunting, dialectical Dr. Watson, whose utter inability to understand what Marx was getting at would provide light relief.

For a substantial advance of

"Hurry up. They still believe we are re-enacting an old Sherlock Holmes adventure."

dinars I will undertake to write the first Sherlock Marx story: "A Study in Scarlet."
PETER SIMPLE